David

The Land of Unlikeness

EXPLORATIONS INTO RECONCILIATION

With best wishes

[signature]

the columba press

First published in 2004 by
the columba press
55A Spruce Avenue, Stillorgan Industrial Park,
Blackrock, Co Dublin

Cover by Bill Bolger
Origination by The Columba Press
Printed in Ireland by ColourBooks Ltd, Dublin

ISBN 1 85607 437 4

Acknowledgements

The members of the Faith and Politics Group for their companionship - some of the material in this book appeared in a number of the Group's pamphlets.

Brian Lennon – a member of the Faith and Politics Group – who showed me his unpublished manuscript *A Future Together: Reconciliation in South Africa and Northern Ireland* (1999).

Byron Bland for showing me two unpublished articles on reconciliation.

John Morrow and André Lascaris for reading various drafts of the text and making suggestions.

Joyce Williams for patiently typing successive drafts.

My wife Mathilde who suggested that this book was my way of coping with the departure of our daughter Naomi to University.

The members of the Corrymeela Community who have put up with me for all these years, and will have to endure more of me as Leader of the Community.

Contents

Introduction

He is the Way.
Follow Him through the Land of Unlikeness;
You will see rare beasts, and have unique adventures.
(W H Auden, *For the Time Being*)

Setting the Scene

This book comes out of living in a divided society that has experienced some level of political violence for all my adult life. But it is not only about Northern Ireland because there are lots of societies experiencing violent conflict, or are recovering from violent conflict. Can such societies make good again? Is the 'elusive quest' (Norman Porter) for reconciliation achievable?

Divided societies provide the backdrop for an important question that is pursued in this book: What can Christian faith bring to the human search for reconciliation? Yes, God was in Christ reconciling the world to himself (2 Cor 5:19) provides us with a beginning and an end to the question, but what about the in-between part? Thus I offer some theological perspectives and reflect on certain biblical texts relating to reconciliation and issues round reconciliation. But first let me tease out what my personal interest in all of this is.

What's Your Interest in This?

'What's your interest in this?' Roel Kaptein, a Dutchman who did a lot of work with groups of Corrymeela members, used to ask. Well, what is my interest in the subject of reconciliation?

A few strands from my family history: My family went to Dublin for a holiday in 1961 and one of my sisters got lost in Clery's store. My mother's first thought was: the nuns have got her. My grandfather on my mother's side signed the Ulster Covenant in 1912 and my mother said of him: 'He would have been a Liberal if it hadn't been for Home Rule.' My grandfather on my father's side played badminton with the local Parish Priest on a Sunday evening. I remember my aunt saying: 'The Catholics are moving into the area'; yet she was a good neighbour to the Catholic family living down the street. I remember a Catholic friend talking about her father being a commander in the IRA in the 1920s; at least one of my relatives was a 'B-Special' at the same time. I remember talking to a Catholic priest who came from the same town as I do. We worked out that we must have travelled on the same bus to school. I have no memory of him, but I can remember the Catholics on the bus crossing themselves when they passed Holywood Chapel and wondering what these strange people were doing. These people did not belong to me. They were not part of my religious or political community.

When I went to school in Belfast in the 1960s, I used to see buses that said 'Ballymurphy' on them. I had no clue where Ballymurphy was. The only contact I had with Catholics in school was through playing chess. The things that struck me about Catholic education – learnt from this contact – was that pupils could smoke and they got beat. Thick hedges screened us from each other.

My father – who was at ease with people of all traditions – was appointed to a job in health and welfare with the help of Nationalist votes – the night before my uncle had a drink with the local Nationalist Councillor. Such was the world before Fair Employment. I can also remember my father going for a job as Town Clerk of Londonderry Corporation, which he fortunately didn't get. My grandfather on my mother's side left his Presbyterian church and went to another because he didn't like the mix of religion and politics – the minister was a Unionist MP and in the Orange Order.

I remember the Northern Ireland of the 1950s and 1960s as being a suffocating place, both religiously and politically. Nothing ever seemed to happen. And there were the silences, the denials, the evasions, the lack of honest conversations – the 'whatever you say, say nothing', the coasting along – a world of profound dis-ease. I belonged, and I didn't belong.

I came to Queen's University, Belfast, in 1966 and my mother pushed me, probably reluctantly, to go to a freshers' conference at Corrymeela organised by the Queen's chaplains. Corrymeela had just been founded a year before by Ray Davey, the Presbyterian Chaplain at Queen's, and I sensed a world of freedom there which I was immediately attracted to. I have been involved ever since.

Ray Davey had been a prisoner of war and was just outside Dresden when the city was virtually destroyed by Allied bombing in early 1945. Out of his war experiences he had two animating concerns: to find new ways of being church – hence his interest in Christian community – and reconciliation. Corrymeela brought these two things together. Ray had a gift of enabling people – particularly young people – to do things. He supplied the vision, the presence and the encouragement. It was a wonderful environment to learn and to take on responsibility. Over the last thirty-six years Corrymeela has certainly enabled me to 'see rare beasts and have unique adventures'. I will mention some of the learning from Corrymeela later.

Corrymeela in the early days was still very much a Protestant world but at least there was a group of people who were seeking to face the divisions in Northern Irish society and were open to meet the 'other sort'. If they hadn't yet fully connected with the Catholic community they were preparing themselves for what was to come in the 1970s.

I worked for Corrymeela in Belfast for a couple of years after leaving university in 1973. I then went to work for the Irish Council of Churches – a body that brought together the main Protestant Churches and some of the smaller ones. Bill Arlow was the Secretary and he had been instrumental in the setting up of the Feakle Initiative which had involved a meeting of Protestant clergy with members of Sinn Féin and the Provisional IRA in December 1974 in a hotel at Feakle, Co Clare – the hotel is still living off the memory. An IRA ceasefire had followed.

Bill Arlow was an interesting and courageous man from an evangelical Church of Ireland background – he had once appeared on the same platform as Ian Paisley. He had all the best qualities of that background – sincerity, conviction and genuine piety – without the bad. He was able to get alongside all sorts of people, including loyalist and republican paramilitaries. He certainly saw rare beasts and had unique adventures in his peacework and it was inspiring to see a person take genuine risks. In retrospect, he may not have realised all that he was involved in, or being used for, but that goes with the territory.

The Irish Council of Churches also had other people of gen-uine substance – Jack Weir, Clerk of the Presbyterian Church; George Simms, Church of Ireland Archbishop of Armagh; Eric Gallagher, a former President and Secretary of the Methodist Church; Stanley Worrall, former Headmaster of Methodist College – were some of them. A number of them had been in-volved in Feakle and they were ecumenical pioneers – certainly George Simms and Eric Gallagher were ecumenical statesmen.

In the late 1960s and early 1970s the Council had been in-volved in pioneering relations with the Roman Catholic Church. This was to lead to the first Inter-Church Meeting in 1973 – at an-other hotel, near Ballymascanlon outside Dundalk. The coming together – at least into the same orbit – of Protestant and Catholic worlds was not without its tensions. All of this was happening as the Northern Ireland community fell apart. I was an observer of all of this and later a participant as I helped to service some of the joint Protestant/Catholic structures and working parties. Relations between the churches, at least at leadership level, have been transformed over the last 30 years. The development of these relationships has taken time, which is one of the lessons for reconciliation work. And without relationships nothing is possible.

One of the things that Bill Arlow and his predecessor, Ralph Baxter, had been involved in from 1973 was taking groups to Holland. These were groups that could not easily meet in Northern Ireland. In 1975 this work became formalised as the Dutch Northern Irish Advisory Committee and I became in-volved in doing some of the administrative work.

These conferences included clergy groups, neighbourhood groups, paramilitaries, police officers and politicians (not all to-gether). The two key people on the Dutch side were a Dominican priest, André Lascaris, and a Dutch Reformed minister, Aat van Rhijn, who had also run an adult education centre. They were to be joined in 1981 by Roel Kaptein (of whom more later). This work had considerable impact on me (and others). It showed a way of working with adults using their life experiences and the importance of providing a safe space where people could learn from each other.

As the 1970s went on, it was clear that taking groups to

Holland increasingly did not make sense and we needed to 'ul-sterise' the work. A decision was taken to work with organis-ations in Northern Ireland. The organisation we had most success with was Corrymeela. There were a number of reasons for this. Firstly, I was chairperson of the Corrymeela Council at the time. Secondly, there was a new leadership team in place at Corry-meela – John Morrow had just become Leader in succession to Ray Davey, and Derick Wilson had been in post as Centre Director for a year or so. The third factor was totally unexpected – the appearance of Roel Kaptein on the scene.

Roel Kaptein had just retired from a senior position in the Dutch Reformed Church. He was one of the bluntest men I have every met: 'Tell me what is your interest in this?' 'Tell me Mr Bishop …' – he once said to an actual bishop, 'Tell me …' He was also one of the brightest men I have ever met; he was a trained psychotherapist and he had just encountered the thinking of René Girard. From 1981 Roel took us 'through the Land of Unlike-ness' and we certainly saw rare beasts and had unique adven-tures until his death in 1996. He had a profound influence on me and many Community members and staff. He changed our style of work. He combined 'head' work and 'heart' work in a unique way. We worked on our questions; we told our stories, and he would stand no evasion or messing around – 'Why does this matter to you?' 'Tell me your story.' He worked with a flip chart, he drew diagrams; we worked for a week at a time, morning and evening – 'O Daddy, you are not going there again.' At the end of 15 years I had learnt a little about relationships, peace and rec-onciliation – and about my evasions, denials and hypocrisies.

Roel, along with André Lascaris, introduced us to the French literary critic, René Girard. Girard, among many things, is a wonderful reader of texts, including biblical texts. He brought ideas about rivalry, scapegoating, conflict, violence and the birth of culture which have profound implications for peace and rec-onciliation work. Girard also provides important insights into how to understand the biblical message and the uniqueness of Jesus. He opened up a view of the world which I find enormously exciting. I have not been the same since.

Roel's method of work created Corrymeela spin-offs. One of these was the Understanding Conflict Trust which Derick Wilson,

Duncan Morrow (now Chief Executive of the Community Relations Council), Roel and Frank Wright founded. The Trust has done significant work with the police and public bodies, because issues of community relations and peace and reconciliation have to be mainstreamed and not remain the preserve of groups at the margin of the main institutions of society. Which brings me to Frank Wright.

Frank was a political scientist at Queen's University and involved in Corrymeela. He had a truly original mind. In my opinion he is the only person to have come up with an original idea in thirty years of academic analysis of the Northern Ireland conflict. His idea was of Northern Ireland as being an 'ethnic frontier'. I have chosen to translate this idea into the concept of 'contested space' but the basic idea is the same. Frank incorporated his idea into a book called *Northern Ireland: A Comparative Analysis* which looks at a number of 'ethnic frontier' societies. When Frank first encountered Girard's ideas he rewrote the book. Frank was not only an academic; he was a courageous human being. During a particularly tense time paramilitary slogans appeared on a wall near his home. He took a paint brush and painted them out. Frank died tragically young in 1994. I still miss him. During all the political change of the 1990s I would often say to myself 'What would Frank think about this?' Shortly before he died he said 'It's been great.' On the way we need companions who will help us see the rare beasts and share in the unique adventures. Frank, who could be an exasperating companion at times, certainly was that.

In 1983 I became involved in the Faith and Politics Group (then the Inter-Church Group on Faith and Politics). The group began when a motion was passed at the 1983 Greenhills Ecumenical Conference calling for the setting up of a Christian Centre for Political Development to analyse the relationship of churches to politics in Ireland. A steering group was set up and a number of people co-opted in an individual capacity. It quickly became clear that a centre was not a realistic goal and the best role for the group was as an unofficial think-tank.

The group has produced a whole series of publications since 1985 dealing with issues of faith and politics. We wrestled with the meaning of political events such as the Anglo-Irish Agreement.

One of the turning points in the group's work was during the production of its first document, *Breaking Down the Enmity*, when we sat down and talked about our personal fears and enmities. Suddenly things got real and a relationship was established between us which involved an acceptance of difference and different perspectives, and enabled us to do constructive work together. We were in a small way a laboratory of reconciliation. Much of the material in this book first appeared in the group's pamphlets.

In the late 1980s I became involved in the setting up of an inter-church Working Party on Sectarianism, co-chaired by Mary McAleese (now President of Ireland) and John Lampen (a Quaker peaceworker in Derry/Londonderry). This was a sensitive project because it was addressing painful issues. Discussion of sectarianism invariably, in my experience, taps into deep personal and group unease. The Working Party, ably marshalled by John and Mary, produced its report. One of the most difficult issues we faced was dealing with the history of sectarianism in Ireland. That was something we could not agree on. The Irish Inter-Church Committee was extremely hesitant about publishing the document – we had discovered their unease. But taking a deep breath, and building on the relationships established over twenty years, it was agreed to publish. *Sectarianism: A Discussion Document* saw the light of day in 1993. The book was only just in time.

Sectarianism became the issue of discussion in the churches in the late 1990s (helped by events at Drumcree). The Irish School of Ecumenics pushed into the gap opened up by the publication of *Sectarianism: A Discussion Document* and building on an earlier Reconciliation of Memories Project, pioneered by the then Director, Alan Falconer. The Moving Beyond Sectarianism Project was established by the new Director Geraldine Smyth and inspired staff were found in the shape of Cecelia Clegg and Joe Liechty. They not only produced the state of the art thinking on the subject *Moving Beyond Sectarianism: Religion, Conflict and Reconciliation in Northern Ireland* (2001) but they did a lot of work with church groups. Sectarianism is a subject that can not be dealt with only at 'head' level; it also involves our hearts and our guts.

Joe and Cecelia's work brought the Irish Inter-Church Meeting and church leadership to a stage of being beyond denial on the issue of sectarianism. Joe and Cecelia would make a presentation and people would ruefully say 'Yes, that's us.' I sought to encourage the project and the Irish Council of Churches provided premises.

The issue of sectarianism – how religious identities and boundaries are distorted, particularly in a divided society – is central to thinking about reconciliation. My reflections on the issue have been guided by the work of Joe and Cecelia.

In the 1990s, new conversation partners arrived on the scene. Evangelicals were traditionally suspicious of, if not downright hostile to, anything that smacked of ecumenism. By extension, anything to do with community relations was off the agenda too. The establishment of Evangelical Contribution on Northern Ireland (ECONI) in 1987 meant that some evangelicals were prepared to engage with others on issues to do with peacemaking and community relations. These were clearly separated off from ecumenism. ECONI's engagement has brought the enrichment and energy of new conversation partners. It has meant that new questions arise, which mean taking the gospel fully seriously. It has also meant facing the question: How do we really make space for others? What has been really exciting is that there is more honest conversation around than ever before.

So what is my answer to the question: 'What is your interest in this?' I suspect my interest in reconciliation is partly rooted in family dynamics – in dis-ease. There was dis-ease at the heart of my mother's family and it communicated itself to me. I hated going to my grandparents' house. In my father's will, drawn up in the late 1950s, he said that if he died he did not want his family to be brought up in that house. He clearly felt the dis-ease as well. I felt the dis-ease of Ulster Protestant life in the 1950s and 1960s: a profoundly dysfunctional society coasting to disaster, all the time vehemently claiming innocence and blaming others. Interest in something is always personal; Roel Kaptein taught me that. I experienced freedom in Corrymeela and that profoundly changed my life, and put it on a different course. So this book is a journey, to find a land of unlikeness, personal, social and political. It expresses some of the learning on the way.

One of the things I have learnt is the importance of story in reconciliation and this is why I wanted to give some personal background – we are 'storied' people – and it is also why I have attempted to give illustrations of what I am trying to say. These are scattered through the text.

Reconciliation in a Contested Space
Words like reconciliation, healing, repentance and forgiveness were until recently largely restricted to the religious domain. As the political scientist Norman Porter comments:

> The intermingling of conventional political and religious languages is one of the striking features of reconciliation's elevation to a political and cultural priority in recent times.[1]

The language of reconciliation is seen to be a richer language than that of justice, particularly in contexts that require a promise of harmony to replace antagonism. For one of the things happening in our world is that conflicts *between* states are being overtaken in frequency and perhaps in importance by conflicts *within* states. The force of globalisation and homogenisation which threaten a sense of community on the one hand, and the (re) assertion of identities – cultural, national, ethnic, religious, social – on the other hand, bring about situations of tension and conflict between communities. What we get are contested 'spaces'.

The diplomatic procedures inherited from the nineteenth century which were designed to effect reconciliation – or at least political settlements – between States are ill-adapted to deal with the issues of reconciliation within and between communities. Here reconciliation becomes much less abstract and more face-to-face. People who have been deeply hurt, whose loved ones have been killed and devastated by injury, actually have to come to terms with the presence on their streets of individuals who did these things to them. It is not surprising that in this context issues like prisoner release and the decommissioning of paramilitary weapons cause significant difficulty. We need to learn about the possibilities and dynamics of reconciliation because of the increasing incidence of conflicts within States. We also need some clarity about what is meant by reconciliation and this is partly what this book is about.

In contested 'spaces' we are always trespassing against each

other. We live with the 'other' in a mutual fear-threat relationship. We easily become caught in a cycle of conflict in which the
actions and behaviours of one set of participants reinforce the
actions and behaviours of the others, and the conflict keeps
going. The result is a deep-rooted insecurity, antagonism and
enmity, and identities shaped by conflict and violence. Communities are caught in destructive patterns of relating together.

In contested 'spaces' there is the danger of reciprocal community violence and the endless cycle of revenge. Frank Wright
had a deep insight into what happens in contested spaces. One
of his insights was that, by and large, national communities that
co-exist on the same soil develop in rivalry with and antagonism
to each other. The result was conflict and such conflicts did not
normally end up with reconciliation of the antagonists. More
commonly they were concluded by final victories or forced sep-
arations. The outcome of the conflict in the former Yugoslavia in
the 1990s is a classic example – Frank Wright predicted the outcome before his death in 1994. Thus, those who espouse a politics of reconciliation in a contested space need to do so in a spirit
of sober realism.

Dealing with the Past
A political settlement is about ending reciprocal community violence and the cycle of revenge through creating a justice system
and institutions that have the consent of its citizens. While there
is an indispensable political dimension to breaking cycles of
vengeance, politics on its own is not enough. This is where the
issue of dealing with the past – the legacy of hurts vividly remembered, the emotional and spiritual woundedness of people
– arises.

All sorts of ambiguities exist about guilt and responsibilities
for past violence. Normally the courts deal with the individual's
guilt for particular acts, but what about individuals who are acting for, or representing, collectivities or whose actions are an
outgrowth of their group malignancy or of society breakdown?
How the past is to be dealt with by societies in transition is of
vital significance, but complicated issues are raised.

Societies in course of transition have to struggle over how
much to acknowledge, how to deal with perpetrators, victims

and bystanders, and how to recover. The American writer Martha Minow says:

> A common formulation posits the two dangers of wallowing in the past and forgetting it. Too much memory or not enough; too much enshrinement of victimhood or insufficient memorialising of victims and survivors; too much past or too little acknowledgement of the past's staging of the present; these joined dangers accompany not just societies emerging from mass violence, but also individuals recovering from trauma.[2]

There are a whole series of potential goals for societies responding to collective violence:[3]

- overcome communal and official denial and silence about the past and gain public acknowledgement;
- seek to memorialise the past and educate about it;
- obtain the facts in an account as full as possible in order to meet victims' need to know, to build a record for history, and to ensure minimal accountability and visibility of perpetrators;
- end and prevent violence; transform human activity from violence – and violent responses to violence – into words and institutional practices of equal respect and dignity;
- forge the basis for a domestic democratic order that respects and enforces human rights;
- support the legitimacy and stability of a political accommodation or a new regime;
- promote reconciliation across social divisions; reconstruct the moral and social systems devastated by violence;
- promote psychological healing for individuals, groups, victims, bystanders, and offenders;
- restore dignity to victims;
- punish, exclude, shame, and diminish offenders for their offences;
- express and seek to achieve the aspiration that 'never again' shall such collective violence occur;
- build an international order to try to prevent and also to respond to aggression, torture and atrocities.

What is important to note is that there are tensions between many of these goals. Further, some are focused on the past, some on the present, and some on the future. Much of this book, and in particular Chapter Six, is taken up with discussing some of the issues involved.

The traumas of the past century have led societies to approach their past in different ways: by repression (Japan, Ireland after the civil war and until recently France); by confession (Germany, South Africa); and by institutional ritualisation of remembrance (Israel). Some of these different ways and their implications will be discussed later. However, it is important to note that we should not assume, at this stage, that the best or only way to approach a reconciliation process is through first establishing what happened in the past which then makes it possible to live together in the present, so that we can move together into a positive future. Elements of the past, present and the future (and the goals appropriate to each) are likely to intermingle in complicated ways in particular situations. What will be argued is that it is necessary to deal with the past at some stage.

It is also important to note that the transition from inter-community conflicts to sustainable peace requires a minimum of ten to fifteen years, or longer. Societies coming out of long and violent internal conflict experience problems every bit as serious as those experienced at the height of the conflict. Change can be a difficult and painful process. Transitions precede transformations. Thus, people need patience and to be sustained by hope: hope that situations can and will be transformed and renewed, that life can and will be changed, and newness can and will come.

Looking for a Way Out

People have a fundamental need for security. In societies governed by fear-threat relationships, wisdom suggests that security comes from deterrence or getting your retaliation in first or from the decisive act of violence or from living among your 'own'. We all know about the threat *from* the 'other'; much harder to acknowledge is the threat we pose *to* the 'other'. Conflict situations generate endless justifications, blame and self-righteousness. There may, however, come a time when significant sections of different communities are ready to find a way out – they can be helped by key parties to the conflict stepping back and co-operating together and facilitating positive movement. The international community may also have a vital part to play.

When we begin to suspect that conflict or the present situation cannot give us what we need or hope for or is unsustainable, then we are open to the possibility of looking for some other way. When it becomes clear that neither force of arms nor force of numbers will get us what we want, we may be open to find another way. These *kairos* moments have to be seized and confidence-building steps entered into. These moments have also to be patiently waited for – and planned for. There is a quiet work of laying in place the building blocks necessary for future action.

Looking for another way means that we need to find a solution with the people with whom we are in conflict. Fundamentally this means facing the reality of the situation and giving the 'other' recognition, respect and acceptance. We stop making people fit into our version of peace. They have interests, fears, aspirations and need for security which have to be taken into account too.

Albie Sachs, a former ANC activist and now a Supreme Court judge, describes a process in South Africa where first there was an increasing recognition that change was needed. A second component of the change was the growing ability of people to learn 'to look into each other's eyes' and acknowledge the fears and needs of the other. Sachs suggested that all were forced to recognise the common humanity that people shared, and he believed from this a growing understanding and mutual respect developed between people who had hitherto been adversaries.[4]

A real peace process requires a partner. As Shimon Peres, former Foreign and Prime Minister of Israel, said of the Palestine/Israel conflict:

I think what is really important for a peace process is the creation of a partner, more than a plan. Because plans don't create partners, but if you have a partner then you can negotiate a plan.[5]

Similarly, Nelson Mandela said of F. W. de Klerk:

To make peace with an enemy, one must work with that enemy, and that enemy become your partner.[6]

Thus we need the 'other' to find peace. We have to develop a relation with those with whom we are in conflict. We have also to be as inclusive as possible in the search for peace.

Politicians have a vital role in moving communities forward. They are figures who represent communities with all their concerns, hurts, fears, enmities and aspirations. At its best this can mean a politician accepting responsibility for the well-being of a community. The German sociologist Max Weber, in his essay 'Politics as a Vocation'[7] speaks of politicians requiring above all 'trained relentlessness in viewing the realities of life, and the ability to face such realities and to measure up to them inwardly'. This facing of reality and acceptance of responsibility for a community's future can mean reassessing a community's position and seeking to find new ways forward, leading to new political agreements. Politicians can help bring 'frightened people across a great divide'.[8]

Practical utilitarian necessity may push a war towards a political settlement. But practical utilitarian necessity will only take us so far; for no lasting peace is possible without reconciliation. We have to be willing to look, with the people with whom we are in conflict, for the ingredients of a reconciliation that may be achieved down the road. These ingredients will involve issues of a refusal of revenge, justice, forgiveness, truth and repentance, and attempts to heal and overcome enmities and to build trust and relationships. Some of the issues involved are discussed in Chapters One and Two.

Moving communities forward has all sorts of dynamics. The suasions of self-interest can be a factor in developing co-operative relations. The Civil Rights campaign, led by Martin Luther King in Birmingham, Alabama in 1963, persuaded the economic leaders of the town that there had to be changes in employment practices and this led to new relationships (black capacity for generosity and forgiveness and white repentance played their part as well).[9] The coercive power of the State can be a factor; for instance, part of the activity of Martin Luther King was to force the federal government into decisive action. Nationalists in Northern Ireland, similarly, fought to make the British government act decisively. The action of Fair Employment legislation, backed up by government coercion, has brought virtuous activity.

It is true that a greater element of justice can come into a situation without repentance or forgiveness. The emollient operation of economic prosperity can ease division, e.g. this has been suggested to be the case in the South Tyrol with its ethnic division between German and Italian speakers.[10] What is being argued is that more is required.

The Religious and the Political
The fact that there is an intermingling of religious and political language as regards words like reconciliation, forgiveness, repentance, trust and healing is interesting. It may even be significant. It doesn't of itself show that concepts and language developed in a religious context bring 'value added' or a distinctive contribution to a political context. Nor can the faith conviction that God was in Christ reconciling the world to himself be directly equated with a political policy and objective. Clearly reconciliation as a human and social process and quest requires theological reflection, because as the South African Reformed theologian John De Gruchy says:

> If there was ever a theological theme that had to be developed in relation to the world in all its agony and hope, this is that theme.[11]

Certainly the faith conviction that God was in Christ reconciling the world to himself requires to be embodied in the life of the church. It would be expected that this faith conviction would have social consequences. It would be hoped that there would be a Christian contribution to the human search for reconciliation – and that this might come from theology, from the life of the church, and from the practice and activities of individual Christians. Perhaps one of the central insights that Christian faith brings is that relationships matter, that they break down constantly, and continually have to be restored. And that brings me to the meaning of reconciliation.

CHAPTER ONE

The Meaning of Reconciliation

Introduction

'Reconciliation' has a particular resonance in situations that have undergone extensive conflict where we need to make good again, e.g. in South Africa with its Truth and Reconciliation Commission, and in Northern Ireland where the logic of reconciliation is intrinsic to the Good Friday Agreement.[1] However, reconciliation's meanings and possibilities vary considerably. We have to be attentive to particular situations.

It also has to be admitted that the word 'reconciliation' has been shamelessly misused to slide away from issues of injustice and rightful disturbance. It has been used to quieten people down and lead them away from the reality of their situation. Use of the word can disguise a lack of political specificity. Archbishop Rowan Williams says '"reconciliation" is such a seductively comfortable word...'[2] But 'reconciliation' can be misused in other ways. There are forms of 'reconciliation' which are about making people fit into predetermined 'solutions'. There is also a tendency in discussion about 'reconciliation' to downgrade differences. Not all differences are reconcilable. A discourse of reconciliation can also be used to suppress pain and trauma and express a wish for a happy 'ending'. And finally, a discourse of reconciliation can appear to claim too much in contexts where getting people into the same room together can be an achievement.

However, I want to rescue the word from vacuity, false comfort and misuse, and to discuss its meaning using six different approaches:

- seeing reconciliation as living together in difference;
- seeing reconciliation in terms of the inter-related dynamics of forgiveness, repentance, truth and justice;
- seeing reconciliation as a place – where the different conflict-

ing parties meet and face together the claims and tensions between truth and mercy and justice and peace;
- seeing reconciliation in the context of revenge and sacrifice;
- seeing reconciliation in terms of a set of attitudes and practices that are necessary for dealing with plurality, for fair interactions between members of different groups, for healing
divisions and for finding common purposes; and
- seeing reconciliation as creating and sustaining conversation.
Most of these approaches overlap. What is not assumed is that
there was a time in the past when the parties were not divided
and there were positive relationships. It will also become clear in
the discussion that reconciliation is much more than peaceful co-
existence. Co-existence is basically an agreement to proceed on
parallel tracks. Reconciliation does not deny difference but speaks
of continuing relationship and partnership.

LIVING TOGETHER IN DIFFERENCE

Reconciliation can be seen in this approach as being able to live
together in difference. The model is of reconciled diversity.

Living together in difference and diversity – racial, cultural,
social, religious – is an increasingly challenging issue facing
today's world. It raises profound issues about community, identity, recognition and how we meet the 'other'. Often there is dis-
ease in the presence of difference and differences have been
dealt with by belittling, dehumanising and demonising, over-
looking, avoidance (polite or otherwise) and by making people
fit in (sometimes through overt pressure). The possibility of people having real meetings where there is honest conversation, respect and mutual regard is narrowed in such situations and they
become hostage to wider communal fears. For instance, there is
evidence that Bosnia's earlier tradition of tolerance was based
only on a politeness which sought to preserve stability.

All group identity is created by encountering what is different. Such an encounter involves a recognition of the 'other'. A
recognition of the 'other' can be positive, but it can often be
based on fear and mistrust and/or a sense of superiority, as the
following example shows.

The former Bosnian President Biljana Plavsic pleaded guilty
to war crimes in October 2002 at the International War Crimes

Tribunal in The Hague. A former biology professor, she borrowed terms from her biology text books and told the Serbs that they were racially superior to the Muslims, and eradication was a natural process. At her sentencing hearing she asked the question, 'Why did I not see the truth earlier?'[3] Her response was: 'The answer is I believe fear, a blinding fear that led to obsession, especially for those of us for whom World War Two was living memory that Serbs would never allow themselves to become victims … At the time I convinced myself that this is a matter of survival and self-defence …' The victimised become victimisers and the aggressors see their actions as self-defence.

Identities can be mis-shaped by recognition or its absence. A group of people can suffer real damage and real distortion if other groups or society around them mirror back to them a confining or demeaning or contemptible picture of themselves.

The institution of slavery in the USA systemically demeaned the humanity of blacks and profoundly affected their identity. A black archivist and curator of a repository for African-American history says in Erna Parris' book, *Long Shadows: Truth, Lies and History*:

I have yet to find a psychological study about the impact of the institution of slavery on people. About how one who was considered chattel, non-human, had to, and still has to, constantly try to convince another group of people that I am human. People sometimes don't understand that when a sports-caster recently said about a black athlete, 'Boy, he runs like a horse', then referred to the white athlete as intelligent – well, that sends shock waves. I think we haven't started to look at the ramifications of dehumanisation. You saw the ship's inventory that lists a person like a bag of spices and herbs? There is not a face or mind attached to that. It's a piece of cargo. You know, I think it was [W.E.B.] Du Bois who talked about oneness and twoness, that there is a constant battle within the black person to strive for oneness – oneness meaning that he is human, twoness, that he is perceived as not being totally human. The black person somehow strives to prove that he is human and it is an ongoing battle within. Even today.[4]

Distortion and damage is mutual in a society of antagonised division. Shame and guilt will be passed down to later generations.

The identities engendered in such situations are often negative identities, based on opposition to the 'other', e.g. through most of European history, Europe defined itself against the 'Turk', Arabs and Islam. President Slobodan Milosevic drew on this history when he told the Serbs of Kosovo in 1989 that 'never again would Islam subjugate the Serbs'. Asserting such identities also serves to increase an awareness of difference and separateness. An identity politics of antagonised division often emerges. Plurality and heterogeneity within the group must give way to homogeneity and unity. Everything must be made pure, with the 'impure' and the different expelled.

Negative identity involves a need to abuse the 'other', often emerging out of one's own experience of abuse, fear, loss or powerlessness. If the rule of positive identity is 'love your neighbour [the 'other'] as yourself' (Lev 19:18), then the rule of negative identity is 'do unto others what they have done unto you, or do it unto them first'. What the Serbs did under Milosevic's leadership in the 1990s in the former Yugoslavia clearly illustrates this. Under the guise of the Bosnian Moslems being the clear and present enemy, one of the prime motivators was to humiliate the other side for what was done in the past: 'We will do to you what your ancestors did to us.'

One of the deepest resistances to peace and reconciliation in many situations is the stubborn commitment on all sides to the negative identities formed over and against others. We need our enemy because of the identity this oppositional 'other' gives us. We may desperately seek to continue the conflict because we cannot envision ourselves in a future that would include positive relations with the 'other'. We need to keep the old 'story' in place. Periods of transition are particularly difficult for identities formed in opposition and this may drive people to more desperate violence as they seek to keep the old world intact.

For transitions to go in a good direction, there needs to be a movement away from constructing identities over and against others, to developing identities that through positive relationships respect others and leave room for difference. People need to have the confidence to engage in a journey that explores who they are and what they might become. This involves a new recognition of the 'other' and a willingness to enter new worlds – a journey of re-imagination and the making of new stories.

The Duality of Difference

The presence of difference generates energy; that energy can be negative and destructive, but it can also be positive and creative. The duality of difference is ever present. The scapegoating and driving out of the 'other' – polarising 'us' against 'them' – is always there as a possibility. However, living together in difference, without domination, opens up the potentiality of creative relationship and dynamic interaction, and a more enlivening future for everyone. Key is the acceptance and even the enjoyment, of difference. The seeking after the 'purity' of sameness is the way to impoverishment.

Covenanting Together

'Covenant' is a central biblical concept, referring as it does to the relation of God to the world: 'God's covenant means a gracious commitment on the part of God to heal and restore God's relationship with the world so that it might be brought to perfection.'[5]

The idea of covenant can be misused. It has been used in Northern Ireland and Scottish history as a way of mobilising opposition against enemies rather than as a way of establishing relationships. The Solemn League and Covenant for Ulster of 1912 (modelled on the national covenants of the 1500s and 1600s whereby Scottish Calvinists joined together, under God, the causes of church and nation in resistance to popery and prelacy, i.e. Catholicism and Anglicanism) was used to mobilise opposition to Home Rule. The Covenant used the phrase *'using all means* which may be found necessary to defeat the present conspiracy to set up a Home Rule Parliament in Ireland' (emphasis added). The Covenant Day

> was essentially a holy day; work ceased and the day began with congregations meeting for worship. Thus were combined together religion, politics and the threat of violence.[6]

Similarly in South Africa the traditional Afrikaner story was of a covenant made between God and the Voortrekkers on the eve of the Battle of Blood River in 1838. The Voortrekkers pledged to God that they would remember the day as a holy Sabbath in perpetuity if God granted them victory over the Zulu army. The event became the key to the interpretation of Afrikaner history during the decades of the twentieth century, celebrated as the Day of the Covenant. The covenant became a cornerstone of the ideology of apartheid. It provided a divine justification for maintaining a separate Afrikaner nation, for the policy of apartheid and the entrenchment of white power.

While the idea of covenant can be misused, and we cannot directly use the idea of a divine covenant in the social and political arenas, nevertheless it is of central importance for people seeking to live together.

The German philosopher, Hannah Arendt,[7] was clear that there were two primary requirements for people to live together: (1) the willingness of people to be bound together by promises and agreements, and to keep them, i.e. they create a covenant together; and (2) the willingness to set aside the past – its enmities and the vicious circle of action and reaction – and start anew; this is where the possibility of forgiveness and reconciliation arises.

Making a covenant together is an attempt to create partnership without dominance or submission. It does not assume that the parties are equal in power. Covenants exist because people are different and seek to preserve that difference, even as they come together in a continuing relationship. The covenant together requires a mutual making space for the 'other'; which may mean redefining identities, in the light of the other's presence.

A covenantal relationship goes beyond social contract, because it is concerned with reconciliation rather than mere coexistence, as was recognised by Nelson Mandela when, in his inauguration address as President of South Africa in May 1994, he declared:

> We enter into a Covenant that we shall build a society in which all South Africans, both black and white, will be able to walk without any fear in their hearts, assured of their inalienable right to human dignity – a rainbow nation at peace with itself and the world.

The willingness of people to be bound together by promises and agreements, and to keep them, is necessary for order and trust in human life. But the imperfection and sinfulness of people mean that we frequently fail to keep promises and agreements. Therefore, we have to find some way of repairing covenants by setting aside the past with its failures and enmities. Forgiveness therefore is a vital component of social healing, of rebuilding relations and creating trustworthy and sustainable structures.

THE INTER-RELATED DYNAMICS OF FORGIVENESS, REPENTANCE, TRUTH AND JUSTICE

I want to argue that for reconciliation to take place there has to be the presence of justice, truth, forgiveness and repentance. What proportion of each of these elements is present in a particular situation is a matter for detailed investigation, and what the implications of this are for the quality of the reconciliation achieved is again a matter for investigation.

The meaning of justice, truth, forgiveness and repentance is developed in greater detail at other points in the text. At this juncture, however, some preliminary clarifications are in order.

The Meaning of Justice
The different meanings of justice include:

Punitive justice	-the punishment of wrongdoers;
Structural justice	-aimed at the structural inequalities of society;
Restitutional justice	-which seeks to make amends by providing reparation for victims;
Legal justice	-directed to the reform of law, the judiciary and policing.

The Meaning of Truth
The different meanings of truth include:

Factual or forensic truth	-legal or scientific information which is factual, accurate and objective and is obtained by impartial procedure;

Personal and narrative truth	-the stories told by perpetrators and, more extensively, victims;
Social truth	-the truth generated by interaction, discussion and debate;
Healing and restorative truth	-the narratives that face the past in order to go forward.

Truth involves truth-telling and truth-learning, and is suffused with moral judgement.

The Meaning of Repentance

Repentance means stopping what we are doing; recognition, examination and acknowledgement of wrongdoing; accepting responsibility; expressing remorse; seeking forgiveness; and seeking to repair the harm done.

The Meaning of Forgiveness

Forgiveness involves letting go of the past (including letting go of vengeance), acting lovingly towards a wrongdoer, and the possibility of a new relationship with the enemy/perpetrator. Letting go of the past does not mean that a justice claim is abandoned (see below).

Forgiveness and repentance have a collective and communal aspect which interacts with the personal and individual.

The Relationship Between Justice and Repentance
Joseph Leichty says:

> At the heart of repentance is always a justice claim, but one of a particularly important kind – it is a justice claim that we acknowledge against ourselves. Repentance involves the uncomfortable awareness that injustice is not solely something we suffer, but also something we inflict, and in this way repentance offers an antidote to the self-righteousness that so easily accompanies the pursuit of justice.[8]

A further link between repentance and justice is that an element in repentance is putting wrongs right.

The Relationship Between Forgiveness and Justice
Joseph Leichty says:

Forgiveness is linked to justice in several ways. As with repentance, there must always be a justice claim at the root of
forgiveness, otherwise there is nothing to forgive and the
language of forgiveness should not be used. But the genius of
forgiveness is to offer a way of pursuing justice, without
being destroyed by the frustration and anger of repeated failures. Forgiveness also helps to ensure that the recompense
involved in justice claims will be directed towards restoration rather than sliding into revenge. This bias towards
restoration brings new options and room to manoeuvre into
the pursuit of justice. Because forgiveness focuses so clearly
on restorative justice it allows the possibility that I may settle
my justice claim by demanding less than full recompense, or
perhaps none at all if that might aid restoration.[9]

Thus forgiveness does not give up on accountability or justice
claims, nor necessarily on punishment.

The Relationship Between Truth and Justice
Justice and truth are forms of acknowledgement and accountability. In truth-telling and truth-learning, wrong-doing and injustice are publicly recognised and acknowledged. What has
happened is brought to light and is faced. There is a weak form
of accountability. The pursuit of justice requires truth because
truth is required to find out what happened, to (re)-establish the
dignity of the victim and the responsibility of the perpetrator. In
justice there is a strong form of accountability.

The Relationship Between Truth and Repentance
Truth-learning (I recognise what I have done) and truth-telling
(I acknowledge what I have done) are key aspects of repentance.
Truth in reconciliation has to be understood in terms of the lies
that wrongdoers perpetrate and the untruthfulness that is creat-
ed,[10] and how these are overcome.

The Relationship Between Truth and Forgiveness
Forgiveness involves knowing and facing what has happened in
the past in order to become free of it. We need some encounter
with the truth in order to have freedom from the past and to be
able to forgive. In fact we cannot fully forgive if we do not know
who the perpetrator is.

Justice in the Context of Reconciliation

This is a perspective which places justice in the context of reconciliation. What is being argued is that the overarching framework is reconciliation, not justice. The demands of justice do not trump all other concerns. This does not mean that justice is unimportant. The contrary is the case, for justice is indispensable to reconciliation. Nor does it mean that in some situations the priority should not be on justice, liberation from the oppressor and regime change. Nor is it being suggested that in contexts of oppression the oppressed should simply forgive the oppressors without a change in the situation. In some situations forgiveness – in its political aspect – is not appropriate. What is being argued is that a perspective of justice is not enough; it has to be placed within 'a more overarching agenda of reconciliation',[11] which is the search for a new relationship. Seeing reconciliation as being built on the inter-related dynamics of forgiveness, repentance, truth and justice makes most sense in the context of a political settlement; a political settlement provides the 'space' in which reconciliation may take place.

Full repentance and full forgiveness, or the rectification of all the injustices perpetrated during a protracted conflict, or a shared agreement about the truth of the past and its painful interactions, are not likely to be fully achieved. However, if each side comes to a better understanding and empathises with the other side, and some elements of repentance, forgiveness, justice and truth are present at the individual, community and political levels, there is a chance to end the conflict and establish peaceful co-existence – a patchwork quilt of reconciliation. In some cases a deeper reconciliation may emerge over time.

THE PLACE CALLED RECONCILIATION

'Mercy and truth are met together; righteousness and peace have kissed each other' (Psalm 85:10, Authorised Version).

This text brings two paradoxes together and embraces them: that the claims of truth and the claims of mercy may conflict; and that the claims of justice (righteousness) may conflict with the claims of peace. The tension between the moral demands of justice and the political requirements of peace have been very clear in Northern Ireland with the early release of politically-motivated prisoners, and in South Africa with the granting of amnesty to those that had been involved in murder and torture, provided only that they were politically motivated and that they made public confession of them. There are tensions between wishing to let go (and even forget) the past – which mercy may seem to require – and the longing for acknowledgement of wrong, the demand for accountability and the validation of painful loss and experience – which the demands of truth may seem to require. Further, although it is not expressed in the text from Psalm 85, there is a tension between mercy and the claims of justice. People may see that mercy in the form of generosity – particularly if it is reciprocated – may be the way forward, indeed the only way forward. However, there is a distaste for treating generously those who have behaved badly – it violates a sense of fairness. Justice in its punitive form demands the punishment of wrong-doers and it seems to violate justice when wrongdoers are re-leased early and included in how the society is governed and in how justice is to be determined. There is also a tension between the demands of truth and the requirements of peace – some of which is discussed in Chapter Six. All of this echoes the tensions between the potential goals for societal responses to collective violence identified by Martha Minow in the Introduction. It is not surprising that peace processes and journeys to reconcili-ation are characterised by ethical unease.

John Paul Lederach[12] suggests that the place called reconcili-ation is where the different conflicting parties meet and face to-gether the claims and tensions between truth and mercy and justice and peace. I have suggested that there are further ten-sions between truth and peace and mercy and justice. All of this is expressed in the diagram opposite.

Such an approach makes it clear that reconciliation is always taking place within a particular context and with regard to a particular set of political and social realities. It also suggests that reconciliation cannot be pursued without the conflicting parties facing each other. For only then can they speak to and hopefully hear each other. What happens in that space between them be-comes the critical issue. Thus, reconciliation is a process of social conversation between the parties and it is a quest. Because it is these things there is no formula for reconciliation that, if imple-mented, will automatically lead to success.

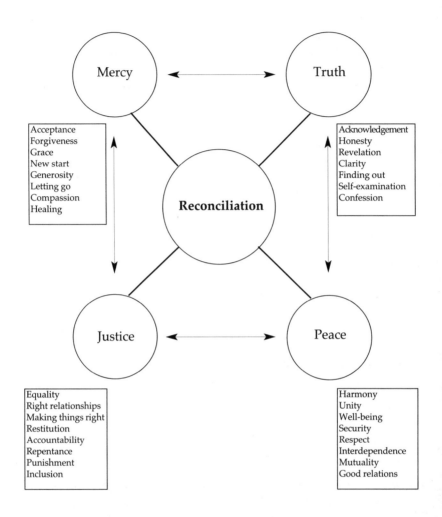

REVENGE AND SACRIFICE

It is important to understand the moral obstacles to reconciliation. The chief obstacles are the desire for revenge and loyalty
to the heroic sacrifices of the past. Revenge and sacrifice are inter-
related forms of respect for the community's dead. Reconciliation
requires new forms of respect which break the spiral of inter-
generational vengeance and loyalty to heroic sacrifice.

Revenge

Revenge is a desire to keep faith with the dead, to honour their memory by taking up their cause where they left off; the violence is a form of respect for the community's dead. Time and again the slaughter inflicted by one side in Bosnia in 1992 was repaying a slaughter in 1942.

Revenge is also an expression of the demand that things must be put right. A wrong has been done and it must be put right through inflicting suffering on the other(s). Thus at the heart of revenge is a demand for justice and this is something we cannot give up. Justice is fundamental to human life: because it says 'I matter.' The use of violence is a way of settling the account and redressing the wrong. We pay back the injury received, for the need for retribution is something deep in us – it appears to express 'fairness' and making things right.

There is, however, a paradox at the heart of revenge. The past cannot be undone. Killing will not bring the dead back to life. The impact of injustice on past generations cannot be undone. The violent pursuit of justice and visions of justice creates more injustice and intensifies the cycle of revenge. And the cycle of revenge brings unending futility.

Sacrifice

The heroic sacrifices of past generations – often founding events, e.g. 1916 in the Republic of Ireland – are another pull of the past on the present, requiring honour and respect. Further, they may require – indeed demand – further acts of sacrifice in the present, because the imagined community of the martyrs must be kept faith with until final redemption is obtained. Nationalisms and political ideologies tend to take on aspects of religion (e.g. 'For God and Ulster', 'For God and Ireland'). As such they make absolute claims on their adherents. In particular, they demand that adherents must be prepared, if necessary, to die for the cause. Memory is renewed by the quasi-religious re-enactment of past events and the glorious dead are made present again. Forms of communion with the dead are created.

Vengeance and sacrifice share much – they are often inter-related. They require – and continue to require – acts of violence, thus continuing the vicious cycle of violence. Violence is sanctified in the commemoration of the glorious dead in stories, rituals and monuments. And commemoration often stimulates further vengeance and sacrifice.

New Forms of Respect

I have argued that revenge is a form of respect for the dead and a seeking after justice. But revenge usually results in an unending cycle of violence and the 'fact' of injustice cannot be undone, e.g. the dead cannot be brought back to life. Therefore cycles of revenge must be replaced: at the political level by an effective and acceptable criminal justice system; with new forms of respect for the dead (e.g. finding out what happened to the dead and where the bodies are, and rituals in which communities once at war learn to mourn their dead together); by exchange of stories and memories which keep people free from violent obsession and revenge; by forgiveness, mercy, forbearance, magnanimity, and generosity; and by forms of justice which do not seek to return 'like' for 'like' (e.g. restitution).

There is a wonderful example of some of this in Michael Longley's 1994 Sonnet *Ceasefire*, which takes a scene from the last book of the *Iliad* when King Priam, desolated by the death of his son, goes to Achilles' tent to beg for the return of Hector's body. Not only has he killed his son, Achilles has mutilated the corpse by dragging it behind a chariot. Further, Achilles has been maddened with rage and grief by the death of Patroclus. But Priam abandons his pride and his fear and begs Achilles for the body and for a proper funeral. The reconciliation that follows was only possible because Priam let go of his 'right' to vengeance:

I go down on my knees and do what must be done
And kiss Achilles' hand, the killer of my son.

Achilles, moved by Priam's appeal and by memories of his own father, mingles his tears with those of the old King and himself dresses Hector's body for the return to Troy.

What is happening is that connection is being re-established across boundaries of antagonised divisions caused by violence. This connection can take a variety of forms and this is illustrated by Anwar Sadat's address to the Israeli Knesset in 1977. Without changing his position in any substantial way, Sadat touched the

Israeli people. He used metaphor, image, the event itself, emotions, and even himself, to link Egyptian and Israel within a common 'we-ness'. He incarnated magnanimity and generosity, as did Nelson Mandela in South Africa. When Mandela first met F. W. de Klerk he immediately made the point that he understood the Afrikaners' suffering during the Boer War.

Similarly, violent sacrifice needs to be replaced by acts of 'living sacrifice' (Rom 12:1) which refuse to victimise others, such as working for justice, peace and reconciliation. The story of what happened after the murder of Amy Biehl is one example:

Amy Biehl was an American girl who was killed by militant black youth in a black township of Cape Town because she was white, although she had gone there to help their cause and was working with the African National Congress. Four black youths were tried and convicted for her murder. Linda and Peter Biehl contacted their families and set up a relationship with them, acknowledging thereby that both sets of parents were powerfully hurt by what had happened and making reconciliatory moves to the others in this way. The youths then applied for and were given amnesty by the TRC and so were released from jail. The Biehl family did not oppose amnesty. Rather they set up the Amy Biehl Foundation to improve life in the black townships where the youths came from who had killed their daughter. This foundation is currently running programmes

• in the environment (the Gugulethu Community Policing Forum, and Mural workshops),

• in education (support for educationally challenged adolescents after school, weekend tutorial programmes, afterschool care programme, family literacy programme),

• in health (safe sex education and AIDS prevention, first aid training),

• in employment (job skills for male adolescents, a community bakery), and

• recreation (developing sports fields, a golf driving range, and a music programme).

Two of the convicted youths approached them for assistance with the Thosanang Youth Club that they wished to set up. On Saturday, July 10, 1999, this club started with support from the Biehl Foundation, which was thus supporting the attempts of two of Amy's killers to better life in their community.[13]

They are now employed by the Foundation.

RECONCILIATION AS A SET OF ATTITUDES, HABITS AND PRACTICES

Seeing reconciliation in this way points to the reality that certain character virtues among citizens are required for the achievement of a reconciled society.

Some of these character virtues are:

- just dealing with others,
- forgiveness,
- empathy,
- respect for others,
- hope,
- patience,
- respect for truth,
- welcoming acceptance of participation in a world of difference,
- willingness to open up to and engage with others who are different,
- honest, committed encounter with others,
- a willingness to work together with others, and
- a willingness to embrace.

We need habits and ways of living that support reconciliation in all its dimensions and build patterns of constructive and co-operative relating together. We need people who teach us the craft of reconciliation. We need places that can provide the experience and skills necessary for us to meet across traditional divisions and deal constructively with difference. It is not enough to 'know' (ideologically, theologically, intellectually) about trust and reconciliation; we need places where people can experience trust and reconciliation, that is where character virtues are embodied in lived relationships. Such places can be family, friendships, organisations, faith communities, centres of reconciliation, schools. Habits and ways of living that nourish reconciliation also need to be mediated and supported through social institutions and public policy that promote sharing and a common space.

RECONCILIATION AS CREATING AND SUSTAINING CONVERSATION

The word 'conversation' would have been understood in the past in a broader sense than is normal today; for instance, the poet Milton spoke about the 'chiefest and happiest end of marriage' being 'meet and happy conversation', understood not as talk but life itself.

The word 'conversation' comes from the Latin verb *conversare*, which means to live together with connotations of habitual proximity and co-operation.

We can understand the work of reconciliation as being that of breaking out of 'the circular arguments of reprisal' (Martin Amis) to create and sustain the conversations necessary to make living together (again) possible. Such activities may involve the 'speech acts' of forgiveness, apology and promises (see Chapter Two), the understanding of different worlds, facing the reality of 'otherness', dealing justly with others, and finding and creating commonality.

In society relationships between groups have to be negotiated, which is a key task of politics. Good politics is the art of conversation. Stable institutions are of vital importance because they provide the possibility of social conversation – the negotiation of difference and living together.

THE POLITICAL MEANING OF RECONCILIATION

Political reconciliation is not just about the accommodation of different interests and aspirations in a mutually acceptable way, although this is important. Political reconciliation in a strong form requires at least three things:
- fair interactions between members of different groups;
- the overcoming of antagonistic divisions and the discovery and creation of common ground; and
- the presence of a society in which all citizens have a sense of belonging.

A reconciled society requires that all its various voices are heard. It requires policies that promote fairness and citizens who act fairly.

A reconciled society is one that has dealt with its destructive divisions through dealing with the past, through giving sufficient recognition to difference and through shared commitment to common goals and a common space. We achieve commonality both through our difference (e.g. in a discovery of our inter-relatedness) and despite our difference (through the things we hold together). The quest for commonality can only succeed if it recognises difference rather than denies difference. However, difference should be recognised in such a way that builds bridges and increases mutual understanding. And differences require the shelter of 'the protecting arch of a legitimate legal order.'[14]

A reconciled society is one in which all citizens enjoy a sense of belonging by having their dignity affirmed at individual, cultural and political levels of their lives. Belonging is tied to institutions with which all citizens can identify and feel loyal to.

None of this, of course, tells us whether political reconciliation is possible in any particular situation. Nor does it tell us anything about the balances we need to strike in any particular situation between the need to treat people fairly, the need to treat people differently, and the need to create shared values and social cohesion. Relationships between groups have to be negotiated, which is a key task of politics. It also has to be done through new ways of working, organising and meeting with one another.

This is a very broad brush approach to the political meaning of reconciliation. But how do we start along a path that might lead to a reconciled society? When enemies begin to suspect that the situation cannot give them what they need or hope for, or is unsustainable, then they become open to the possibility of finding a way out. That means finding a solution with the people with whom they are in conflict. The enemy has to become partner. But enemies seek the destruction of each other's way of life and by definition the enemy is a foe who must be eliminated. The start of a political reconciliation process requires, therefore, not only a 'realistic' discernment that a way out is required but also a cognitive shift of seeing the other group not as 'enemy' but as 'adversary'. An adversary still requires to be contended against, but in a non-violent way. There has to be a move from war to politics and it may take some time for the precise boundaries between war and politics to be established (as in Northern Ireland). Shifting from 'enemy' to 'adversary' requires a mutual

letting go of enough anger, pain, antagonism and suspicion so
that some sort of productive relationship is established (there is
an element of mutual forgiveness here), for the adversary has
also to be partner. We have to find some way of co-operating
and living with our adversary, because we cannot achieve what
we want without their assistance, for they are not going to go
away, and *vice versa*. The writer and broadcaster Michael
Ignatieff says of the reconstruction of the famous bridge at
Mostar in Bosnia and the co-operation between Moslem and
Croat to make it possible: 'So let's not talk about some grand
spirit of reconciliation. Let's just say people are getting practical.'[15] They need each other.

A relationship has to be negotiated that involves former enemies starting to view and act towards each other as trustworthy
political partners even in the face of continuing disagreement
and conflict. Byron Bland calls this 'agonistic partnership'.[16]
Beyond this a more positive reconciliation dynamic may develop.
Such developments are usually protracted, torturous and often
very difficult.

RECONCILIATION AND TRANSCENDENCE

To speak about transcendence is to speak about something 'beyond' or 'above' the contesting parties. In religious terms this is
the presence of God; thus reconciliation takes place in the presence of or through a third 'party' ('He is the peace between us.'
Eph 2:12). A reconciled society requires the creation of a secular
'transcendence' – a common authority, a legitimate legal order,
which is 'above' or 'beyond' individuals and particular groups.
Common authority can be embodied in institutions (e.g. Parliament or the Monarchy) or in constitutions (e.g. the American
Constitution).

RECONCILIATION AS GOAL, QUEST AND PATH

In the earlier discussion, reconciliation has been treated as goal,
quest and path. I have indicated that the goal (a reconciled society) is not some final state of harmony and unity. There is always
an eschatological reserve; reconciliation in its fullness always
lies beyond us. And reconciliation is a quest because there is no
formula, which produces 'reconciliation'.

I have also indicated that reconciliation can be seen as a path and that certain moments and events can help us along that path. John De Gruchy highlights the importance of certain 'events and moments' that are both intimations of what reconciliation means and catalysts for taking the process further.[17] He instances the release of Nelson Mandela from prison as such an event and his inauguration as President of South Africa as a remarkable moment, as were the days South Africa won the World Rugby Cup and later the African Football Cup of Nations.

Along the path of reconciliation might be a commitment to bring an end to violence; we might then have a sustainable peace. Building a future in which different groups feel secure is another step. Ending injustice is important. Learning to co-operate together and co-exist may be other steps. Dealing with the past will become possible at some stage. A willingness to change or repent is part of the process of reconciliation and when this appears another stage has been reached. Forgiveness may become a possibility. The development of greater sharing and integration may be another stage. But it is always work in progress.

RECONCILIATION AND HEALING

Healing is a way of understanding reconciliation and the metaphor of healing is often applied to post-violence situations. The healing paradigm casts the consequence of collective violence in terms of trauma, sickness, brokenness, hurt and pain. A whole society has been gravely wounded and the goal is recovery and restoration to 'health'. Further, an analogy is being drawn between the psychological and physical needs and the therapeutic responses appropriate to individuals and issues involving entire groups of people and even societies.

Some of the limitations of this metaphor need to be understood. To talk about the needs of particular victims is fully appropriate but, for instance, healing is an absurd notion for those who have died. Not all the wounds inflicted can be healed. To talk about an entire society recovering from the consequences of violence has its appropriateness but we need to appreciate that this is fundamentally different from the personal healing process. For instance, a country and its politicians may be ready to move on long before victims have come to terms with what has happened to them. Further, the metaphor of healing has no necessary connotations of dealing with forgiveness, repentance, justice and truth. No specific acts are required by anyone. It is a much 'softer' approach to reconciliation, unless we extend the metaphor to the 'cleaning' of the wounds.

Another area in which we use the healing paradigm is in relation to a belief in the healing power of truth. Not only do we apply this to individuals (the dysfunction of repressed memories) but also increasingly to collectivities. The belief in the healing power of truth was at the heart of the Truth and Reconciliation Commission in South Africa which was established with the hope that it would lead to social catharsis: the revelation of truth about the past would bring reconciliation. But as the Israeli philosopher Avishal Margalit says, 'memory breathes revenge as often as it breathes reconciliation and the hope of reaching catharsis through liberated memories might turn out to be an illusion.'[18] I have suggested earlier that we should see reconciliation in terms of a dynamic interaction of repentance, justice, forgiveness and truth. It is too simple to just see reconciliation in the context of truth. I will further discuss some of the (complex) issues in relation to truth in Chapter Six.

In Conclusion
Reconciliation means people finding a way of living together in difference. It involves the restoration of broken relationships. It requires wanting the 'other' to be with us and not wanting to destroy, dominate or separate from them. It entails being able to take others into account and sharing power, responsibility and resources. It makes us go beyond the 'right' and 'wrong' of the conflict – the vicious circle of action and reaction – to create new, creative and just relationships. It is the painful forging of a shared world. Reconciliation takes time, 'slow and painful time' (Stanley Hauerwas). Reconciliation is not some finished Utopian state. It does not abolish conflict or the friction of living together. It may be and often is partial and incomplete; and it does not remove the intransigent presence of evil.

Reconciliation is not just about an accommodation of various interests and aspirations in a mutually acceptable way. It is concerned with the social reconstruction of a society and thus it is also connected with the rebuilding of the moral order.

Reconciliation involves social transformation: it deals with the hurts, resentments and enmities that exist (the task of repair and healing) and seeks the transformation of relationships with all that implies at the spiritual, psychological, social, economic and political levels. Reconciliation requires *metanoia*, a conversion of mind and heart. It demands particular attitudes and practices. An understanding of reconciliation is necessarily built on the inter-linking dynamics of forgiveness, repentance, truth and justice. It deals with the past, seeks to find a way of relating to the 'other' in the present, and looks to the future. Reconciliation takes people to a new place. And finally, reconciliation is a place – a space – where the different conflicting parties meet and face together the claims and tensions between truth and mercy and justice and peace. It is a dynamic quest.

CHAPTER TWO

More about Forgiveness

Forgiveness has multi-layered aspects and much confusion is caused by eliding them and slipping between them. Further, the difference between forgiveness and reconciliation is frequently confused. This chapter is an attempt to offer some clarity.

The Different Aspects of Forgiveness
In being injured, a person is caught up both with the injury and with the perpetrator and what they have done. Talking about forgiveness in this context has a number of aspects:

- *A letting go of vengeance.* This does not mean letting go of a justice claim. It may mean the justice claim being settled by a less than full recompense, by apology, etc. It does not necessarily preclude punishment. But in whatever form there will be an acknowledgement of a justice claim, of an offence.
- *A letting go of those feelings, especially hatred, that will damage, either immediately or eventually, the wronged party.* The wronged party has to overcome the suffering caused by the deed and to re-establish the ability to trust. If violence is involved, a person's whole sense of being in the world may be threatened – the 'lie' of violence can coil into the innermost recesses of a person. Suffering erodes the meaning the individual has about their life and the world. For the person to become whole again they have to work their way through the violence and this may involve anger and protest and lament against what has happened. It may mean the person finding a new narrative to make sense of themselves and the world.
- *Acting lovingly towards the wrongdoer* (the equivalent of 'Bless those who persecute you: never curse them, bless them', Rom 12:14). Gordon Wilson illustrated this after his daughter, Marie, was killed by the Remembrance Day bomb in Enniskillen in 1987 when he said in a radio interview the

same night that he bore no ill-will to those who had killed his daughter. Further, for years he tried to meet with the IRA to express personally his desire for an end to violence (a meeting he was eventually able to have). Acting lovingly may take the form of praying for the other's good and for restoration. It may involve feelings of empathy for the perpetrator. This aspect of forgiveness may be similar to love of enemies. Such love has nothing whatever to do with having nice feelings towards wrongdoers. It springs from a deep knowledge that some measure of the humanity of the perpetrators has also been lost – and that they need to be redeemed too. Acting lovingly can open the way to repentance (in the case of the prodigal son, the father's love produces repentance, as does Jesus' love for Zaccheus) but it is not guaranteed.

- *A speech act[1] of forgiveness ('I forgive you').* This is an important point in letting go and is normally but not always preceded by a long journey. Often the speech act of forgiveness will be preceded by repentance by the wrongdoer. This may not always be the case; sometimes forgiveness comes first. The speech act of forgiveness says the same thing ('I forgive you') but means different things in the two circumstances.

    In forgiveness preceded by repentance it means: In the light of your remorse and acceptance of guilt and responsibility, I let go my full justice claim on you and hope that we might start anew. As we move to full reconciliation, I trust that the remaining issues between us can be sorted out.

    In forgiveness before repentance it means: I take the risk of letting go my full justice claim on you in the hope that you might repent and that we might start again. I further hope for a full reconciliation in which the issues between us can be sorted out.

The second circumstance is much more difficult than the first and is illustrated by the experience of Frank Chikane, former General Secretary of the South African Council of Churches. In the late 1970s he was tortured by the security police. On occasions he was beaten so badly that he could not walk. The policeman who tortured him was subsequently promoted to a senior post and under the 1993 Agreement was able to retain his job. In the course of his work he met Chikane several times after the transfer of power but at no stage did he offer an apology. His lack of apology was in marked contrast to the behaviour of a former minister in the National Party who came up to Chikane and said: 'I am very sorry because I was a deputy minister of law and order when you got detained. We ordered that, and I know you were tortured and I know we were wrong, and I want you to forgive me.' Chikane comments: 'I find it very difficult to relate to him [the policeman] in the way that I would relate to a person who has confessed …'[2]

Forgetting

Forgiveness is not forgetting. Forgiveness requires some recognition of the offence; forgetting is an omission, the offence is no longer important. Forgiveness offers a certain kind of remembering – a 'good' remembering not a 'bad' remembering. Janet Morris puts it this way:

> Bad or unhealthy remembering is the kind which broods over the wrongs suffered, stoking up hatred of the other and refusing to look at any possible wrong in the self, or any interpretation of events but one's own. This will harm the 'rememberer'. However, good remembering is a realistic and healthy way of dealing with the hurts of the past. In this, nothing is denied or frozen into repression; feelings and actions are acknowledged, but choices are made not to be bound by them – to absorb them and move on, open to the possibility of restoration and a new future. Inherent in this is a loss of innocence about human relationships, but also a growing maturity in handling them; a maturity which can face up to pain and acknowledge loss, but also see the possibility of moving through it to deeper and richer friendships with other human beings – and with God.[3]

There may also be a certain kind of 'good' forgetting; forgetting not as amnesia but rather as a release from the full weight and burden of the past. In restored relationships there are some things that no longer matter.

Forgiveness involves coming free of the power of the past and finding ways to a different future and is usually a long and difficult journey. A journey of forgiveness involves different dimensions: words (spoken and unspoken), actions (made and not made) and emotions (felt and overcome). Forgiveness is often discovered, not willed. Stories of forgiveness and repentance may help, as may the liturgical and community life of the church. A third person – a 'go-between' person – may also open up a space for new possibilities to occur.

Forgiveness is not Reconciliation

There is a difference between forgiveness and reconciliation. Forgiveness is our side of the process: we forgive someone who has injured us. Only we can forgive; no one can do it on our behalf. It may and often does lead to reconciliation. But not always. Why? Because the other party may not say 'sorry', may not repent, or may not be willing to accept our forgiveness.

Repentance means turning and changing one's ways. The person who commits wrong has to do more than say 'sorry'. He or she has to turn towards the person they have wronged, acknowledge what they have done, accept responsibility, express remorse and try to make amends. It involves a willingness to enter into new and just relationships. Repentance, like forgiveness, rarely happens at once. It is important to keep space open for little glimpses of repentance and change, for repentance involves risk and vulnerability.

I have also argued that truth and justice are involved as well. Reconciliation only happens when forgiveness and repentance come together, and the claims of justice and truth have been faced. In this process the status of both victim and perpetrator change, and as their relationship is re-negotiated they become different people. This is confirmed by research done on the Truth and Reconciliation Commission in South Africa.[4]

An Illustration: The Story of Ginn Fourie

Ginn Fourie's daughter Lyndi was murdered in the 'Heidelberg Tavern Massacre' in Cape Town, South Africa, in 1993, six months before the first democratic elections. The four men who committed the shooting were members of the armed wing of the Pan Africanist Congress. Fourie noted several stages on her journey 'from tragedy to healing':

- owning the feelings of excruciating pain, grief and loss of Lyndi;

- accepting the graciousness of God's forgiveness and love in her own life;
- somehow absorbing the violence of Lyndi's death, which she sensed as a miracle;
- feeling empathy for the prisoners in their fear and confusion at the criminal trial;
- offering forgiveness to Lyndi's killers, who she regarded as evil men;
- episodes of direct communication with the perpetrators, where she tried to be honest about her pain and fears and listened to reasons for their hurt and hate;
- the perpetrators' acceptance of responsibility for the hideous crimes which they had committed and their apologies;
- the perpetrators' gracious act of accepting her forgiveness and the healing for everyone, symbolised by embracing; and
- lastly, a vision for reconciliation on a larger national scale.[5]

Ginn Fourie links at the end forgiveness in the area of inter-personal relationships to forgiveness in the political realm, and it is to that that I now turn.

Forgiveness and the Political

Individuals cannot be compelled to forgive or repent, even if there is a communal disposition towards forgiveness and repentance, a political settlement broadly acceptable to a large majority of people, an end to violence and a move towards societal justice. These may facilitate interpersonal forgiveness and repentance, but they do not guarantee it. Some may not repent and others may not be able to forgive. Not all the ends can be tied up. Thus we have to make room for the unforgiving and the unrepentant.

We have to distinguish between interpersonal forgiveness and political forgiveness and also between different categories of victims. Victims can be divided into three groups which correspond to different levels of suffering:

- Primary   -   those who have suffered direct injury.
- Secondary -   family and friends of primary victims.
- Tertiary   -   the wider community, political society itself.

Interpersonal forgiveness belongs much more to the primary and secondary levels, political forgiveness to the tertiary.

Political forgiveness is a process within a society involving political action, and makes particular sense in a context of political agreement, but it also operates in 'normal' politics (see below). The American ethicist Donald Shriver argues[6] that a process of political forgiveness is marked by forbearance from revenge, empathy for opponents, concern for moral truth, and a desire for positive co-existence. These are things that politicians can encourage and in some cases do. I will show in Chapter Six that politicians in some situations can representatively express repentance and, in particular, apologise. It is less clear that politicians can representatively forgive. They can encourage forgiveness, by showing mercy, magnanimity and generosity to political opponents. They can pardon criminals. However, the speech act of 'I forgive (a nation, a community) on behalf of (a nation, a community)' is much more problematic. Forgiveness in its fullest expression is much more personal. However, individual acts of forgiveness can encourage and empower other people to forgiveness as well, so that communities and nations may change. Gordon Wilson's response after the Enniskillen bomb had a restraining effect on loyalist paramilitary retaliation. Nothing, however, is guaranteed.

The State may pardon wrongdoers. For this to remain a form of forgiveness, some recognition of the offence must remain. Otherwise, it is institutional forgetting (see the discussion on the South African Truth and Reconciliation Commission in Chapter Six).

Individuals may also forgive the State, its institutions and politicians for their failure and shortcomings. In fact this is necessary for society to function and for there to be relations of respect and trust between citizens and government. Again for this to be forgiving and not forgetting these failures and shortcomings have to be acknowledged, e.g. through apology.

CHAPTER THREE

Theological Perspectives

Introduction

God has made human beings in his own image (Gen 1:26); all humankind shares equal dignity and is owed equal respect. However, in the biblical vision there is no humanity without relatedness. The image of God in human beings is bound up with mutual inter-relationship and inter-dependence (Gen 1:27). In this picture we are not individuals on our own but persons in community who collaborate with God. This community of persons extends to social and political units. The creation stories in Genesis do not end with the creation of humanity in chapters one and two, but with the creation of the tribes and nations in chapter ten. God is the author of our common humanity and of our diversity.

The first two chapters of Genesis affirm the covenantal relationship of trust between God and humanity and the ontological priority of peace over conflict and violence. However, what follows is the story of the Fall and, leading from it, the beginnings of human conflict and violence. At the heart of this account (in Gen 3:5) there is a primal moment of human mis-recognition: the false and envious perception that God is someone to be rivalled with. This rivalry means that human identity – rather than being given – establishes itself over and against God (and our fellow human beings). Such an identity always has something of violence in it.

The story of the Fall does not conclude with the story of the exclusion of Adam and Eve from the garden; instead it concludes in Genesis eleven with the confusion of tongues at the Tower of Babel and the scattering of the nations, as the nations too rival with God.

Fundamental in the Genesis story is how alienation from

50

God brings a deep insecurity into human affairs. Fear of the neighbour, rather than trust in God, becomes a governing factor in human relations. The neighbour becomes an oppositional 'other' who threatens us. In this insecurity we do two things: we create our own substitute 'gods' or idols, that belong exclusively to us and seem to offer the security we need. And we use our differences from others to give ourselves esteem and identity as individuals or a group. Our group is purer and inherently superior: we are what we are because the 'others' are not what we are – and therefore not as good as us. At the same time they excite our envy, our fascination and our fear. By their presence they question and limit us. These attitudes involve self-deception, mis-recognition of others, self-hatred, hatred of others, rivalry, exclusion and victimisation. Inevitably our victims, when they can, victimise us in return.

So we live defensive lives, dominated by the 'realism' of fear. This realism says that we must always retaliate when offended, that we must always look for revenge, that we must always be ready for war, that we must dominate or be dominated. If we cannot dominate or eliminate the threat, we may accept the 'peace' of mutual deterrence, or we may separate ourselves from the 'other'. The weight of our threat, or the distance between us and the 'other', become the measure of our security. Such 'solutions' lessen the possibility of violence. Nevertheless they are ways of life based on fear and mistrust of the neighbour. Stories of what the 'other' has done to us, or will do if we don't defend ourselves, become our controlling narratives. Stories of trust or co-operation are forgotten or not believed.

What does Christian faith have to say to this? The gospel offers us an alternative reality to fearful, frozen and defensive living. It invites us to imagine ourselves and our world differently. Reconciliation in Christ takes us to a new place – the house of Christ – where we think, speak and act in his way, where fear becomes trust and hurt permits healing. Christ breaks down the middle wall of partition and invites us all into a space created by him to find people who were previously our enemies. New conversations are opened up with liberating possibilities. The present becomes a place for risk-taking and for participation in the transformation that God is working on the earth.

Encountering the Other

All identity is created in the encounter with the 'other'. Therefore, how we meet the 'other' – give them recognition, respect them, give them a place, find ourselves in them – is a central challenge of all human existence. Further it is a fundamental religious challenge because in the human 'other' there is a trace of the divine 'other' who has passed by already (see Exodus 33).

The Jewish theologian Marc Gopin suggests[1] that the stranger – the 'other' – is the essential metaphor of biblical experience and the key to its ethical stance. The Hebrew Scriptures say that the vulnerable 'other' – including the resident alien and strangers – shall be protected (e.g. Deut 10:18-19; Lev 25). And the reason for this is that the children of Israel themselves are only 'strangers and guests' (Lev 25:23). This is taken up by Jesus in the parable of the sheep and the goats when he says that how the vulnerable 'others' – the hungry and thirsty, strangers, the destitute, the sick, those in prison – are treated becomes a test of our real attitude to him (Mt 25:31-46). Thus we are 'de-centred' from self and our 'normal' home to the world of others. In a fundamental sense the 'other' brings life to us.

The implication of all of this is that we need to relate together in a mode of *pro-existence* in which there is a dynamic and creative relationship connecting and binding all the parties concerned for the benefit of all. Pro-existence makes possible the sharing of a space in a way that offers everyone the possibility of having their identities and traditions acknowledged and given a place. Pro-existence goes beyond mere co-existence, because we need the 'other'.

Belonging

We need distance and we need belonging. Group identities offer us homes in which we can belong: a sense of pride, a space where we are among our own, a place of nourishment and security. And at the same time they can become 'fortresses into which we retreat, surrounding ourselves by impenetrable walls dividing "us" from "them". In situations of conflict they serve as encampments from which to undertake raids into enemy territory.'[2] Thus group identities are profoundly ambivalent: 'havens of belonging as well as repositories of aggression, suffocating enclosures as well as bases of liberating power'.[3]

Cultural and group differences cannot and should not be removed. We cannot live without differences and boundaries – even if we know that differences and boundaries can be dangerous. We can, however, open ourselves to be enriched by our differences. And, at the same time, different traditions, cultures and languages are cultivated. There is respect for boundaries. But boundaries must be porous; the 'other' is to be welcomed in and embraced. There is respect for difference and diversity, but not sectarianism and exclusion. We become 'go-between' people, who can see both 'from here' and 'from there'.

Jesus, while remaining completely a Jew, cut across the boundary markers between Jews and Gentiles. He set aside food taboos. He went into Gentile houses and healed (e.g. the story of the healing of the daughter of the Syrophoenician woman, Mk 7:24-30); he went into the country of the Gentile Decapolis and healed the Gadarene demoniac (Lk 8:26-39); and he engaged in a profound dialogue with the Samaritan woman at the well (Jn 4).

Paul persecuted the early Christians because he felt the sacred boundaries, which made the Jews special, to be threatened. Paul's encounter with Jesus on the road to Damascus changed his whole life. Without wishing to destroy Jewishness, he turns away from an attitude that emphasises sacred boundaries to find a new identity in Christ that excludes none – an identity which has no over against, an identity given by Jesus the Victim. He sees the dividing wall of hostility between Jew and Gentile as being broken down through the Cross (Eph 2:13-16) so that the 'other' can be welcomed in.

A Vision of Embrace

The Croatian theologian Miroslav Volf describes his vision of what should be through the metaphor of 'embrace':

> In an embrace I open my arms to create space in myself for the other. Open arms are a sign that I do not want to be by myself only, an invitation for the other to come in and feel at home with me. In an embrace I also close my arms around the other. Closed arms are a sign that I want the other to become a part of me, the other enriches me. In a mutual embrace none remains the same because each enriches the other, yet both remain true to their genuine selves.[4]

Difference is not the cause of division but the enrichment of unity. But it is a genuine embrace based on justice and respect for truth. Not everything that everybody does is to be accepted uncritically.

Such a vision respects borders and boundaries but welcomes the stranger in. It allows for difference but provides for positive and life-giving relationship. The vision of embrace is an aspect of the love of the neighbour.

A vision of embrace seeks to break out of the vicious circle of seeing the 'other' side as always to blame, and our 'side' as always the righteous, the innocent and the good one. Joe Peake, former Development Officer of Enniskillen Together, describes the following experience:

> Israeli Jews see themselves as victims of Palestinian terror but when, in a relaxed, non-critical atmosphere, they visited an Arab refugee camp they were able (with great emotion) to see their 'own side' was also a perpetrator.[5]

We have to learn that the 'others' are human like ourselves, with a good and a bad side, and people to be lived with, even if we have significant disagreements with them. We need to learn about the threat we pose to and the fear we induce in the 'other'. Indeed, our fears and insecurities help to create and maintain our enemies: 'The judgements you give are the judgements you will get' (Mt 7:1). We are the problem (the beam is in our eye) as well as our 'enemy'. Others, although different, are human like us and worthy of respect.[6] We take them into account and treat them with consideration. They, too, have their fears, interests and desires and, therefore, we should treat them as we would like to be treated by them (Mt 7:12). We do not want to be victims, therefore we must not victimise others. The 'other' is our neighbour with whom we must learn to live.

Embrace is a risk. I open my arms, make a movement towards the 'other' and I do not know whether I will be misunderstood, despised, even attacked, or whether my action will be appreciated, supported or reciprocated. But it also opens the way to surprising encounters, enriching conversation and transformation. And the final act of an embrace is a letting go. The arms must open again. The 'other' remains 'other' and we must continue to 'negotiate' our difference. There is no final settlement of difference.

A CHRISTIAN VISION OF RECONCILIATION

The New Testament shows a God who has a deep solidarity with suffering humanity and who wishes to overcome breakdowns in relationships. The enmity between God and human beings is overcome through Christ's loving embrace of us on the Cross – 'For he is the peace between us, and has made the two into one and broken down the barrier which used to keep us apart' (Eph 2:14). There is a mending of brokenness and we are brought to a new place ('there is a new creation', 2 Cor 5:17) where we are able to make space for the 'other' because Christ has made space for us through his self-emptying (Phil 2:7). And it is God who takes the initiative: 'It is all God's work. It was God who reconciled us to himself through Christ' (2 Cor 5:18). We are called and invited to accept this gift of reconciliation, offered to us in Christ, and proclaim it to the world.

The enmity between Jew and Gentile is also overcome through the Cross – the dividing wall of hostility between different groups of people has been broken down (Eph 2:11ff). We are given a vision of a new humanity, reconciled in Christ, living together in a new community.

While we are made one in Christ, particular identities are not abolished but they are relativised and subordinated. This new identity in Christ leaves no room for individual or collective claims of superiority or self-righteousness. Reconciliation in Christ is about being freed from anxiety about identity. We do not have to shore up our own selfhood or self-esteem. We can stop denying and repressing our guilt. We can trust in the goodness and grace of a faithful God.

God's loving forgiveness opens the way to repentance and prepares the way for reconciliation (for example the story of Zaccheus in Luke 19: 1-10). Issues of justice and truth are not ignored. Thus love operates within a moral order which involves truth and justice.

All of this has social implications. Christians are the visible fruits of God's reconciliation in Christ. They are called to make this reconciliation visible – visible in terms of a quality of relationships, visible in terms of openness and hospitality. It is a visibility which serves the same purpose as Christ's visibility, namely to reveal God and his reconciling love. This is true holiness and is the ministry of reconciliation (2 Cor 5:19).

Healing is a way of understanding reconciliation and there is a rich Christian tradition of using the metaphors of sickness and healing, particularly but not exclusively in Eastern Orthodox theology. Jesus can be seen as the 'wounded healer' (Henri Nouwen) who uses his own wounds to heal the wounded hearts of others – suffering vulnerability becomes redemptive. In this sense, healing is the central part of his mission.

Jesus in his person is the image of God (Col 1:15). In his message, attitude, way of living and being, he brought something into this world that the world could not understand (Jn 1:10) and was profoundly threatening. Jesus protests against a world in which violence is met by violence and where scapegoating, expulsion and exclusion are the norm. He ends on the Cross, an innocent victim. He breaks with the vicious cycle of revenge by absorbing, not returning, violence. The message of the Resurrection is that the destructive powers of the world who resist truth, justice and love, will not prevail.

A Christian vision of reconciliation speaks of something given us, of remade humanity, of renewed and redeemed relationships, of restored community, of the cost of love, of the acceptance of limitation, of suffering vulnerability, of self-emptying love that makes space for others – all in the context of a fragmented world where hatred, enmity, violence and antagonised differences are common, and of a God active in this world mending its brokenness and bringing a new creation. This vision makes us increasingly sensitive to victims, for Jesus was a victim of hatred, enmity and violence.

Politics cannot bring this vision of reconciliation into being. Our faith conviction that God was in Christ reconciling the world to himself cannot be directly equated with reconciliation as a political policy and objective. However, faith in a renewed and transformed world gives us courage to be persons of persistence and creativity seeking to create a new reality in the midst of politics, for we recognise that the world of politics is a place of encounter between humanity and God, and where the knowledge of the world's victims is made present.

Violence demands its victims – its sacrifices. Peace and reconciliation may also demand 'sacrifice', though of a different sort: that involved in a commitment to a loving and non-violent God and in a commitment to stopping the scapegoating and blaming that exists in a devious and violent world. It is a way of 'living sacrifice' (Rom 12:1), living the new world out already, led by the memory of the crucified and risen Lord and the presence of the Holy Spirit.

At the heart of Christian faith is a person who did not make victims and yet was put to death as a guilty one. In the Eucharist we return to this innocent victim ('Do this in remembrance of me'). Through this remembering once again, the past is made contemporary and the liberating activity of God is experienced. The activity of remembrance is paralleled with God's remission of sin, through the death and rising again of Jesus. As we appropriate the memory we are able to accept responsibility and seek forgiveness. We remember that the sacrament originated 'in the same night as he was betrayed'. Those who eat at Jesus' table are his betrayers, then as now. And he continues to accept us, to allow us into his fellowship. We remember the body broken 'for us' who were God's enemies and the blood shed to establish the 'new covenant' – the new relationship of promise and commitment – with us who have broken the covenant (1 Cor 11:24-25). We also partake in the expectation of a new heaven and a new earth ('Until the Lord comes, therefore, every time you eat this bread and drink this cup you are proclaiming his death', 1 Cor 11:26). Thus memory becomes a ground of hope for a redeemed future.

In the remembering of Jesus the liberating activity of God is experienced and we are offered the possibility of remembering the people we have diminished and rejected and injured – the people we have made victims. We are given back memory. This recovery of memory is the ground of hope, for it offers us, in the presence of Jesus, the possibility of the restoration of relationships. There can be no authentic hope without memory.

The Christian story is about giving us the memory – through the innocent victim, Jesus – to see our own victims (this is deep remembering). It is a subversive memory because it makes us uncomfortable, because our false innocence – the narrative we wish to tell – is exposed. We enter a new story where we relinquish denial. We see and accept our part in the story. We discover the truth about ourselves.

The Christian story also tells us that the victims do not in their turn make victims: 'Never repay evil with evil' (Rom 12:17). The aim is the remaking of relationships, the embrace of the 'other', the starting again of promises and commitments, and the ending of revenge for we no longer need to inflict suffering on others. Victims are not required.

CHAPTER FOUR

Reflections on some Biblical Texts
relating to Reconciliation

Introduction

I want to use the resources of the biblical tradition to illuminate issues around reconciliation. In some places I use paintings to illustrate the text. Let me start with three stories from the Hebrew Scriptures which deal with rivalry and conflict between brothers and with various forms of re-union.

Cain and Abel: Protecting the Destroyer – Genesis 4

Cain cannot tolerate the difference that God has made between himself and Abel. He desires what his brother has, and in so doing his brother becomes an oppositional 'other'. So Cain murders Abel in an act of possessive violence. In a sketch by Rembrandt Cain kneels on his supine horrified brother. He parts Abel's defending hands with one arm and raises a jawbone with the other. God in response says: 'You shall be a fugitive and a wanderer over the earth.' Cain finds this prospect terrifying: 'Why, whoever comes across me will kill me.' Therefore, God puts a mark of protection on him: 'If anyone kills Cain, sevenfold vengeance shall be taken for him' (v15). Justice begins when vengeance is choked off; Cain leaves the presence of God, guilty and alone. But he is not exterminated. And, according to the biblical theme of re-union, we are all descendants of Cain, destined for re-union with the descendants of Seth, Abel's substitute (v25).

Therefore, the elimination of one brother is not followed by the elimination of the other. Sanctions are imposed – Cain is cast out from God's presence into the Land of Wandering – but without bringing destruction: the guilty party is given protection against vengeance. A substitute is found for the innocent victim and the possibility remains of descendants being able to live together – a space is held open. But the way towards re-union is not opened up; Cain remains in his limbo. Inexhaustible patience is required in the face of intractability.

The Story of Jacob and Esau – Genesis 30-33
Jacob and Esau are twins and this is a symbol of the conflict that they are going to experience. The idea that twins are dangerous is deep in ancient cultures, because they are often rivals. The two brothers also stand for two nations: 'There are two nations in your womb, your issue will be two rival peoples' (Gen 25:23). Esau, the firstborn son is supposed to be the ancestor of the people of Edom, Jacob will become the ancestor of Israel.

The story of Jacob in Genesis chapters thirty to thirty-three involves a person who wants to be a winner and is a deceiver and a clever schemer. He cheats his brother Esau out of his birthright, and thinks that by being a sharp operator he can find security. And at the same time he is full of insecurity and fear of what his brother will do to him – he is possessed by the dark. It is not, therefore, surprising that Jacob finds himself wrestling with a mysterious figure in the dark (Gen 32). There is both a mysterious figure (an angel?) and a mysterious event. Perhaps the figure is, at one and the same time:

• Jacob and his fears and his past;
• his brother Esau: the person he has wronged; and
• God – for Jacob wishes a blessing, he wants divine approval.
Delacroix's mural *Wrestling with the Angel* makes the event a passionate encounter. Jacob thrusting forward on one leg, bare-backed, locked in an aggressive embrace; the angel, paler, calm-faced, buttressed by a pair of huge and folded green wings with his right hand gripping Jacob's thigh to inflict the wound. It is clearly a passionate encounter, but is it about conquest or testing? Is there a winner and a loser? Is it less a struggle than an embrace?[1] Does the encounter's meaning lie in the outcome or the meeting itself? Is the event full of dread or welcome? Delacroix's mural 'holds' all these meanings.

Yes, Jacob wins, he gets a blessing, but he loses his old identity, his old name. He receives a new name – Israel – and thus a new identity. The story shows that real winning and security are paradoxical. They do not come through clever manoeuvring. Real winning and security involve transformation. And transformation does not come without struggle, conflict, pain and a permanent woundedness (or at least a memory of woundedness). In the story Jacob wrestles to daybreak and his hip is dislocated.

The sun rises. This means that the dark ends for Jacob. There is transformation. He limps towards reconciliation with his brother. The story illustrates that new relationships and reconciliation involve vulnerability.

In chapter thirty-three Jacob shows himself to have changed. He does not put everybody in front of him so as to escape at the cost of his wives and children. He himself goes ahead; he makes himself vulnerable. He recognises Esau as his Lord (seven times). In verse ten he sees in Esau's face the face of God. The blessing he had been trying to get he now gives to his brother Esau. Jacob is not in a hurry any more; he now knows that he should not travel faster than those who are the weakest – the children (v14). Peace has come.

Jacob and Esau are reconciled, but this reconciliation does not mean the two brothers living together in harmony. Instead the two brothers go their separate ways. Reconciliation has meant putting an end to mutual destructiveness and hostility but Jacob and Esau maintain peace by living apart – by keeping a distance from each other and by each of them preserving their independence. There may be a prudence and a wisdom operating here: that if there is too close a relationship conflict may break out again. Each brother needs a clear separation from the other, but this takes place without violence.

We sometimes assume that peace requires togetherness, but this is not necessarily true. Dutch society created peace through the 'pillarisation' of society. Protestants, Catholics and a secular group had their own separate institutions until the 1960s, political parties, trade unions, schools, etc.

The Story of Joseph and his Brothers – Genesis 37-50

In the story, the jealousy of the brothers precipitates a crisis and the expulsion of Joseph from his family. They want to kill Joseph but finally they sell him as a slave to a caravan heading for Egypt.

Joseph, after many adventures, rises to the rank of Prime Minister to Pharaoh. The seven years of famine arrive and there is famine 'all over the world'. But Joseph is able to protect Egypt through his skill in husbanding resources during the seven years of plenty. The ten half brothers of Joseph suffer because of the famine in Canaan. So they travel to Egypt to beg for food. They don't recognise Joseph as Prime Minister in his beautiful garments, but Joseph recognises them. Without making himself known, he inquires discreetly about Benjamin, their younger brother. He has been left at home for fear that some misfortune would happen to him, causing their old father, Jacob, to die of grief.

Joseph gives wheat to all his half-brothers. He warns them, however, that if they come back because of the famine, they must bring Benjamin, or they will get nothing. The famine continues on, so the ten finally return to Egypt. This time they have Benjamin with them. Joseph allows them to buy wheat, but he also has a servant conceal a precious cup in Benjamin's sack. Complaining then that someone stole this article from him, Joseph has their bags searched. When the cup is found, he announces the arrest of the allegedly guilty brother, Benjamin, and he authorises the ten older brothers to return home peacefully.

What Joseph is doing is submitting his guilty brothers to a temptation they know well, since they have already succumbed to it: that of abandoning with impunity their youngest brother, the weakest and most vulnerable among them. Nine of the brothers fall a second time to this temptation. What is going on here? It seems Joseph, at one and the same time, desires reconciliation with his family and cannot forget what his brothers have done to him. His past continues to haunt him. The truth of his anguish has to come out if he really is to forgive, and his brothers must come to know his anguish too. It is Judah who unblocks the situation by offering himself in the place of Benjamin. This profoundly touches something in Joseph; he weeps and pardons all the brothers. In his adopted country, he welcomes and receives his entire family, including his old father, Jacob.

A moment of reckoning occurs between Joseph and his brothers (there is an account, the injustice is named) but it is peaceful, in keeping with Joseph's affirmation of God's providential intentions for Israel and Egypt (Gen 45:1-15). Joseph triumphs; right prevails, his innocence is confirmed. But his triumph is not achieved through revenge but through pardon. The story does not end as it began, with a violent expulsion. Instead it concludes with reconciliation and the inclusion of everyone. The pattern of repetition is decisively broken. The final episode is a profound reflection on violence and, in particular, violent expulsion 'whose radicalism is revealed at the point where pardon replaces the obligatory act of vengeance.'[2] It is only pardon that is capable of stopping the spiral of reprisal – of action and reaction – and the pattern of violent expulsion.

The story also suggests that reconciliation does not come without travail. Joseph suffers, the brothers suffer. There is a journey to reconciliation, which involves a number of different dimensions. In this story there is a literal journey to Egypt. There is a journey in time – in this story decades; and there is a cognitive journey – of discovery and recognition. Finally there is Judah's surprising action – his voluntary willingness to replace Benjamin – that opens the way to pardon. Judah's willingness to become vulnerable and to offer himself as victim touches a man to the depths of his soul who has known vulnerability and victimisation. Joseph is 'given' the capacity to break the cycle of returning evil for evil.

In this story there is complete integration of the guilty parties. We are beyond patience and prudence. The fraternity is re-established which forms the basis for the confederacy of the twelve tribes of Israel.

Entertaining Strangers – Genesis 18

Abraham is the pilgrim-stranger *par excellence*. He left his home and country and set off to an unknown land. He abandoned the stability and prosperity he enjoyed in the land of the Chaldeans, the cradle of civilisation, and became a homeless nomad, vaguely searching for a home not yet known, simply believing in the promise of God (Gen 12:1). Taking his barren wife along, he crossed barren deserts and stayed in foreign lands while sharing with his wife the pain of sterility.

While strangers and nomads, Abraham and Sarah hosted the angels of God outside their tent by the oaks of Mamre (Gen 18). The hospitality of Abraham and Sarah to the three angels became known in Christian theology as the Old Testament prefiguration of the Holy Trinity.

Through the celebrated icon of the fifteenth-century Russian artist Andrei Rublev, the theme of Abraham's hospitality (*philoxenia*, literally 'love of the stranger'), entered the world of Christian art. In the icon of Rublev, the tree representing the oaks of Mamre symbolises nature, the whole of creation and ultimately the tree of life (Rev 22:2), which carries the symbolism of the cross and perfect communion with God. Hospitality is offered and received in the lap of nature, making the creation a partner in the act of communion. This is why it is significant that Abraham received the strangers outside the tent. And, as a stranger invites strangers to rest a while in this particular piece of ground, the place is rendered holy by the communion of hospitality.

The tree behind the three angelic guests conveys a very discreet yet vivid presence, neither dominantly overshadowing the guests and host nor reduced in perspective to the vanishing point. It is the presence of the kingdom of God in its invisible visibility. It is the cross of Christ and the *axis mundi*, (the turning point of the world) linking and reconciling earth and heaven, creation and creator, material and spiritual into one communion (cf Eph 1: 10).

How we 'entertain' the stranger – the 'other' – is a key category of ethical (and biblical) thought. The theologian Thomas Ogletree says, 'to be moral is to be hospitable to the stranger'.[3] The stranger, socially and psychologically vulnerable because he stands outside the network of community reciprocity, needs shelter and food as well as recognition and orientation in an unfamiliar place. However, the stranger, in turn, can offer stories, thus opening up new worlds, and the relationship changes and becomes more balanced. Now the stranger becomes host and the host becomes stranger, having to enter new worlds too. Each becomes 'gift' to each other. For positive co-existence to occur, we have to be prepared to enter each other's worlds.

Of course, we can refuse the interruption and the conversation of the stranger, because the stranger can bring anxiety and indeed contestation. We may not want the 'other' in our world and then we may have to live with the reality that we have refused a messenger from God.

The Sacrifice of Isaac – Genesis 22: 1-19

At the last moment an animal substitute is found for the sacrifice of Isaac. In Rembrandt's print, *Abraham's Sacrifice*, an angel grabs Abraham from behind as he is about to slit Isaac's throat. This text insists on drawing attention to the fact that the animal is a surrogate victim, slain on behalf of a designated human victim. Human victims were probably offered long before animal victims were substituted for humans and Abraham's near sacrifice of Isaac is an allusion to this. The text is pointing to the reality of a victim mechanism – the necessity of violent sacrifice – by which human societies have typically operated.

What does this have to do with us? After all, we are beyond human and animal sacrifice, aren't we?

The work of René Girard[4] suggests that the killing of victims was necessary for the stability and peace of society and at the centre of civilisation is founding murder. This text alludes to this reality too because the substitutional sacrifice of the animal also leads to a founding event. Abraham receives a promise that he and his seed will be blessed (vv16-18).

If culture is born of violence then the artifacts of culture (the arts, painting, poetry) are immersed in violence and fascinated by it. Thus violence is not marginal to the history of European high art – it is at the core of the great tradition.

The very birth of the Renaissance was violent. At the beginning of the fifteenth century, a competition was held in Florence to choose an artist to cast doors for the city's Baptistery. The subject was the sacrifice of Isaac; you can see Ghiberti's winning piece in the Bargello museum, and what sets it apart from Brunelleschi's rival sacrifice is greater and more convincing violence – the sweep back of Abraham's arm as he holds a knife to his son's throat. In the figurative tradition of painting and sculpture, that began with the casting of the dome in the Baptistery in Florence, violence is unavoidable.

Goya's *May 3rd 1808* – perhaps the greatest war picture of all time – is an account of an atrocity in which French soldiers execute Spanish civilians following a partisan attack on French cavalry. What is striking is the brute anonymity of the soldiers. Previously a certain level of nobility and heroism was allowed in war paintings, but there is no nobility in what is going on in this picture. Goya is the last of the Old Masters and the beginning of the modern.

Picasso, perhaps echoing Goya, in his famous picture *Guernica*, learned how to make violence not something the spectator observes passively, but something we experience as if doing it, and suffering it, ourselves. Picasso bombs Guernica. In recognising and making sense of the painted mayhem of *Guernica*, we repeat its violence. As we try to understand the fragments and their relationship, we make things happen. The triangular shapes that surround the screaming figure at the right of the picture are not flames. They are triangles. Only when we decide they are flames does the fire burn.

Guernica is experienced as a succession of epiphanies of violence. The sufferings of *Guernica* are registered in sudden, traumatic recognitions. To burn. To hold your dead baby. Picasso hated war, yet it is by goading imagination to do its violent worst that he shows us what, exactly, war is.

Picasso's painting is, from first to last, a passionate inquiry. He was drawn to violence for the same reason Ghiberti was. It was a means to see more, feel more, know more. Thus, what is being expressed at one and the same time in Picasso's art is the tawdry reality of violence and his (our) profound 'caught-upness' in violence and art's profound 'caught-upness' in violence.

War and our requirement for order need justifying myths and calls upon art to help. The biblical texts progressively unmask the world of violence, particularly sacred violence. This is decisively done on the Cross. The mechanism of substitutional sacrifice is exposed and sacrifice becomes 'living sacrifice' (Rom 12: 1), which is self-dedication to God.

As the gospel works its way through culture, culture becomes deeply uneasy about violence, while still immersed in it. These great pictures are evidence. This uneasiness does not stop us killing, but our justifications become increasingly hard to believe, and our glorifications of violence increasingly shallow. Thus religious and nationalist rhetoric justifying violence has to shout to convince itself.

The Parable of the Prodigal Son – Luke 15:11-32
A couple of years before he died, Henri Nouwen wrote a beauti-

ful book entitled *The Return of the Prodigal Son;*[5] it is both a commentary on Rembrandt's famous painting by that same title and a long spiritual reflection on the fatherhood and motherhood of God. Nouwen points out that, in Rembrandt's painting of the father of the prodigal son, the figure painted there, representing God, has a number of interesting features. First of all, he is depicted as blind. His eyes are shut and he sees the prodigal son not with his eyes but with his heart (to which he is tenderly holding the son's head). The implication is obvious, God sees with the heart. Moreover, the figure representing God has one male hand (which is pulling the wayward son to himself) and one female hand (which is caressing the son's back). Thus God is presented here as both mother and father, loving as does a woman and as does a man.

Moreover, the scene, as depicted by Rembrandt, highlights three characters: the prodigal son, his older brother, and the all-compassionate father/mother figure who is offering the embrace of compassion, forgiveness and reconciliation.

The focus of the parable has normally been on the wayward son who journeys into a far country, finds himself and returns home. However, it is also important to remember the often forgotten older brother who is consumed by anger, resentment, self-righteousness and the refusal of generosity. Why does he have these feelings? Possibly it is because his goodness has not been given sufficient recognition by the father. He would really prefer the father to punish the younger brother rather than welcome him home. The older brother wants to be told how right and good he was, and is (and, of course, in one sense he acted better and more rightly). However, some forms of 'goodness' really need other people to be 'bad'. It may even be that some 'good' people drive others into 'badness'.

What the painting invites us to do is to see ourselves in each of these characters, that is, in the weakness of the wayward son, in the bitterness of the older brother, and in the compassion of the father/mother, God, the God who embraces and offers us a chance to make good again.

In conflict situations there are the sins of people who have journeyed into the far country of violence. There are also the people who stayed 'at home', who remained law abiding but

who have been consumed by anger, resentment, self-righteousness and the refusal of generosity. This parable reminds us
about the sins of the prodigal and the respectable, and the transformation required of everyone.

The Story of the Prodigal Son Revisited[6]

The normal reading of the story is of the prodigal son first re-
penting ('he came to himself'), then confessing ('Father, I have
sinned against heaven and before you; I am no longer worthy to
be called your son') and finally the father forgiving him. The
order is: repentance → confession → forgiveness and the assumption is that forgiveness requires repentance first.

There is another reading of the story in which the central act
is the running of the father to greet the returning sinner. His son
had broken the strict code of the community of which he had
been a part. His request for his inheritance was an insult to his
father and should have led to his banishment for rebellion.
Instead, the broken-hearted father gives him what should legally
have come to him only after his own death. The son promptly
wastes 'his substance with riotous living' (Authorised Version)
and even becomes ritually impure by living among the pigs. He
decides to return home, hoping for a job, but not at this stage
truly repentant. He is simply doing what he has always done –
trying his luck.

In deciding to try his luck at home, however, he will place
himself in great danger, because he must run the gauntlet of the
village elders, guardians of the community's moral code, before
he can get to his father and make his plea for a job. According to
this code he is no longer a part of the community he walked out
of. If the elders see him enter the village, they will break an
earthenware vessel over his head as a sign that he has shattered
his covenant with the community and may henceforth be offered no succour: he is already dead to them. The sorrowful father
sees him before anyone else and runs to meet him. This was in itself an extraordinary break of the patriarchal code, which speci-
fied that the greater your dignity the more slowly you moved.
The father does the unexpected.

The waiting father has no interest in his own dignity or status.
He rushes out to meet and embrace his disgraced child. It is this

abandonment of the correct moral code and of the conditionality of forgiveness being dependent on repentance that is the scandalous heart of the story. The son is clearly forgiven by the father before he can get a word out, and when he does produce his prepared speech there is a significant omission: 'Then the son said to him, "Father, I have sinned against heaven and against you; I no longer deserve to be called your son",' full stop. There is no plea for a job on the farm.

This reading of the parable suggests that the father's outpouring of love caused a true change in the son, so that we might say that the forgiveness that was unconditionally given actually caused the repentance that followed it, an exact reversal of the order that is followed in the usual pattern of forgiveness conditional on repentance. The parable ends inconclusively, because it closes with an act of petulant defiance of the father by the elder brother. Here, again, the father ignores the traditional code by going out to him to explain the nature of his heart's rejoicing at the return of his brother. Since the parable stops at this point, we do not know whether the older son also responded to the unconditional love of the father with a radical change of heart. We do know, however, that this father is not one who makes differences, who establishes categories of reward and punishment, and who sees his sons as rivals for his affection, his prestige and his property. As the parable ends, the focus is on the older son, but both sons have a basic choice to make: will they see themselves in terms of the father's love or not?

The path of conditional forgiveness – repentance, confession, forgiveness – is the path we most commonly follow and see in our daily lives. And there is also the path of unconditional forgiveness. When we see it, or better experience it, we are truly in the world of grace. There have been some wonderful stories of unconditional forgiveness in Ireland. A couple of these are told in Chapter Six.

Showing Acceptance – Luke 15: 3
'This man', they said, 'welcomes sinners and eats with them.'

The importance of accepting hospitality and eating with people echoes through the gospels. Having a meal together is a powerful ritual, as Alpha courses have discovered. Accepting hospitality shows respect and gives dignity. Shared meals were particularly important in Israel. They were a sign of fellowship acceptance and honour. The meal symbolised what the nation should be – a holy nation, maintaining purity and separated from defilement. The meal also anticipated what the nation would be when God acted in power to vindicate his people (see Is 25:6). Meals were bound up with keeping the law – especially regulations regarding purity.

Since the shared meal proclaimed a vision of Israel as a holy people, both in the present and the future, there could be no place at the table for those who were, in the judgement of the Pharisees, neither holy nor pure. Neither sinners nor tax collectors belonged in the holy community. The sharing of meals together or refusing to do so, therefore, had deep religious and social significance for Jews. Table fellowship was a key boundary marker, signing who were in and out of the holy community. Thus Jesus' eating with sinners cuts across and questions boundaries, and challenges an understanding of holiness and community based on purity, separation and exclusion. It also signed and opened up the possibility of a different future where forgiveness, repentance and reconciliation could take place.

Jesus enacts the return of people to the community without demanding that things are set right first and that they change first. This was truly scandalous to the leaders of the Jewish nation and temple. Jesus cuts across the concern that justice be done first. He does not abolish, however, the concern for justice and right living; in the case of Jesus' association with Zacchaeus, he opens up the way to repentance and restitution. Jesus' vision of holiness also scandalised because it was based not on separation and exclusion but on relationship, particularly with the despised, the compromised and the marginalised. Jesus' understanding of holiness reflects the inclusive mercy and love of God that draws people to him rather than makes boundaries.

Some of these themes are illustrated by the film *Chocolat*. The film is set in a small French country town in the 1950s where nothing seems to have changed for generations. The town is held under rigid control by a puritanical mayor who bludgeons the young Catholic priest into keeping a very strict eye on every aspect of people's behaviour. Into this scene, apparently from nowhere, arrives a woman, who is a single parent with a young daughter. She opens a chocolate shop: from there an extravagant supply of chocolate pours – chocolate drinks, chocolate sweets, chocolate cakes, chocolate eggs – and all during the season of Lent. The Mayor is appalled by what is going on: by the disruptions of order, morality, and the transgression of purity that this woman and her chocolate bring. The end of the film comes on Easter Day. The priest casts aside his sermon notes and tells the congregation what he has now learnt: that we should show our love to God by what we embrace, not by what or whom we exclude.

Having conversations with people who are excluded because of their violence can open up the way for new possibilities. The willingness of some church people to meet with republican and loyalist paramilitaries in Northern Ireland has been important. Such activity should not be seen as trivialising violence, nor is it without its ambiguities. In 1985 Father Gerry Reynolds and the Rev Sam Burch – both associated with the Cornerstone Community – determined to visit every dead victim's family, whether the victim was recognised as 'innocent' or 'guilty', and attend their funerals. As Sam Burch recalls, 'Jesus didn't wait until we had repented: "while we were yet sinners, Christ died for the ungodly".'[7]

Who is Really Blind? – John 9

As Jesus went along he saw a man who had been blind from birth and his disciples asked him 'Rabbi, who sinned, this man or his parents, for him to have been born blind?' The community assumption is that for a person to have been born blind someone must have sinned. Jesus heals the blind man and this sparks a crisis, for the miracle is challenging a belief system – a mythology about people. It is impossible for this man to see.

The man is brought before the Pharisees and interrogated, his parents are interrogated, and finally the man is interrogated again. It becomes clear what is at issue is the Pharisees' need to have sinners. Jesus is a sinner, 'For our part we know that this man [i.e. Jesus] is a sinner' (v24) and the man is a sinner,' 'Are you trying to teach us?' they replied, 'and you a sinner through and through' (v34). The community is in order and at peace when there are sinners, i.e. scapegoats.

To believe in Jesus (to really 'see') would involve the end of scapegoating that holds the community together; it would involve the end of 'blindness' – the mythology about sinners. It is not surprising that the Pharisees don't know where Jesus comes from (v29) because it is clear that he comes from a world they do not know about.

As the discussion goes on, it emerges who is really blind, i.e. those who are determined to keep the scapegoating in place. Some Pharisees who were present say, 'We are not blind, surely?' Jesus replied, 'Blind? If you were, you would not be guilty, but since you say "we see", your guilt remains' (vv40-41).

Communities will desperately attempt to keep their scapegoats – 'peace' means that the scapegoats are in order, 'Isn't this the man who used to sit and beg?' (v8). Elaborate mythologies will be built up so that we can remain blind (e.g. 'All blacks are dirty, lazy, etc'). Change will be fiercely resisted – the scapegoats must be kept in place – and violence comes quickly. Violence lurks around this text – 'And they drove him away' (v34), 'They hurled abuse at him' (v28). Reading about the life of Martin Luther King reveals the violent response of many whites in the Deep South of the USA when he and others sought to change the traditional role of blacks. Working for change required incredible spiritual courage.

Do You Want to be Healed? – John 5:1-9

'Do you want to be healed?' This is the question that Jesus puts to the man at the Pool of Bethesda who has been ill for thirty-eight years. It seems a question with an obvious answer – yes, of course. But illness and existence round this pool were a way of life for this man.

We may imagine all sorts of questions going through his head when Jesus asks the question, 'Do you want to be healed?' 'What am I going to be without my illness?' 'What am I going to do?' 'How am I going to earn a living?' 'How will this change my relationship with other people?' 'How will I cope?' A whole crowd of questions milling round demanding answers. And Jesus simply says, 'Take up your bed and walk' and the miracle is he does.

Do people in societies riven by conflict want to be healed?

People who have lived their whole way of life in conflict and violence know where they are with conflict and violence. Having enemies gives identity. There is always someone else to blame and life is really rather secure. Admittedly we are disabled and dysfunctional, but the surroundings are familiar and we know the people. Like Tom and Jerry we are always fighting, but we really need each other, and it would be rather boring without the conflict. The conflict gives us identity and we have a stake in its continuance.

Do we want to be healed boils down to the question: Do we want to change? Change means taking responsibility and finding a new way of living with other people. Real peace means that we have to be different people. Do we want to be? The story of the man at the Pool of Bethesda suggests that Jesus would answer, 'Just do it'. Then we might have a miracle and surprise ourselves. That might make us really interesting – and healthy – people.

The Wounded Healer: The Risen Lord Appears to Thomas
– John 20: 19-29[8]
Even though he has been transformed beyond death, Jesus still bears the wounds of his crucifixion. The first time Jesus appears to the disciples he shows 'them his hand and his side'.

Thomas is absent this first time, and upon hearing the news will not believe it. Only if he can see Jesus and touch his wounds will he believe. The next time that Jesus appears to the disciples Thomas is present. Jesus presents himself to Thomas and invites him to touch his wounds. Thomas replies 'My Lord and my God.' Thomas is brought to faith and trust in a reconciling act on Jesus' part. Thomas is not rebuked for his lack of faith and trust although his doubting is acknowledged. Instead he is invited to touch the wounds. In touching the wounds Thomas is healed – made whole again, forgiven and reconciled.

The wounds make it clear that there is continuity between the crucified and the risen Lord. The memory remains but a memory which has been woven into a new story where the 'lie' of violence has been exposed and where reconciliation will have the final word.

Wounds bear a kind of knowledge – the memory in flesh of

trauma, pain and disruption. Wounds can heal, because having these memories, they can connect to the wounds of others. The transfigured wounds of Jesus have not lost this quality of memory, of crucifixion. When Thomas touches these wounds he touches the memory of his own woundedness, his failure as a disciple, his lack of faith.

The resurrected Jesus knows of healing – as well as trauma, pain and disruption – and that 'knowing' communicates to Thomas. Thomas can reconfigure his life in a confession of faith and trust. Thus people who have been wounded and received some measure of healing themselves can often be the best healers. In conflict situations, victims and ex-paramilitaries who have learnt something can often play the most constructive role.

Reconciliation through the Common Enemy – Luke 23:12
In the passion story recorded in Luke, Jesus is brought before Herod, treated with contempt, made fun of, dressed in a royal cloak and sent back to Pilate. Then the text says: 'And though Herod and Pilate had been enemies before, they were reconciled that same day.' It is through their common enemy, Jesus, that Herod and Pilate become friends.

When a nation or community is divided against itself, it can unite by waging war on or opposing another nation or group. A common enemy has been found and it is one of the most powerful ways of producing internal reconciliation – and politicians have a deep knowing about it. Anglican and Presbyterian were brought together in nineteenth century Ulster through a shared opposition to gaelic, catholic, nationalist Ireland. Often what appears to hold secular and religious groups in Israeli society together is a shared opposition to the Palestinians and to the Arab nations.

It is not surprising that the winding down of wars often produce internal difficulties in groups and communities. The reconciliation produced by the common enemy is basically a variant of the scapegoat mechanism – the mechanism that evokes unity in the face of conflict and division by finding a victim, a guilty one, that can be expelled.

The peace Jesus brings and the reconciliation between Jew and Gentile (see Eph 2: 11-22) is very different from the friendship and reconciliation between Herod and Pilate: 'Try then to imitate God as children of his that he loves, and follow Christ as he loved you' (Eph 5:1).

This is a peace and a reconciliation built on loving one another (in social terms, showing respect) which implies, on the one hand, accepting that the other person is different and, on the other, accepting we share a common humanity. The refusal to scapegoat is the beginning of true reconciliation.

Finding Another Story: Encountering the Risen Lord on the Road to Emmaus – Luke 24:13-28

After the resurrection, on the Road to Emmaus two of the disciples meet the risen Jesus but cannot recognise him. They remain blinded by religious/nationalist expectation because they had all along fundamentally mis-recognised him: 'Our own hope had been that he would have been the one to set Israel free' (v21). Jesus had failed because he had not ended the Gentile domination of Israel.

The disciples are enabled to recognise Jesus by two things. The first is through the retelling of the story of the history of Israel by Jesus – and they had to enter this story again, this time with the risen Lord at the centre of it. The second is in the breaking of the bread, in the communion of hospitality. The memory of the table fellowship – and the disciples' relationship with Jesus – is recreated in this act. Even a cursory reading of the gospels highlights the importance of meals in the community life of Jesus' disciples. We have glimpses that bread breaking and table fellowship were an integral part of the formation they received. Further, the experience of sharing food was profoundly connected with the gift of hospitality and with a recognition of God's presence among them.

The risen Lord returns as stranger, having been killed by the religious and political powers, given up by the crowd and abandoned by all. It is the stranger who finds the disciples on the road – disillusioned, blinded by religious and nationalist expectation, deserters of Jesus – and enables them to find their lost selves. Thus the risen Lord comes in acceptance, mercy and forgiveness. The disciples are loved into new life.

Neither are we lost in our betrayal of him: in our complicity in victimisation, exclusion, violence and structures of sin. Jesus is alive; he is there to be encountered again, to be learnt from afresh. Part of the learning can derive from our recognition of this complicity – whether active or passive – and our awareness that we are, in various ways, 'crucifiers'. Thus we are led to humility and repentance.

Further, the betrayals and failures of the disciples did not set the agenda for the future. Jesus rose above all these things and went before them into Galilee. He invited the disciples to join him there, to go into a new future. So we too can go into a new future. Past failure does not disqualify us from going into a new future. We need, however, to be given and enter a new story, a story not based on the old religious/political expectation. To move towards a reconciled society means that we have to be given new eyes and ultimately be remade, to become different people.

Truth and Reconciliation on the Damascus Road: The Conversion of Saul – Acts 9: 1-20

The story of Saul and his conversion makes it clear that some people will resist the Spirit of truth (and the change it represents) and seek to persecute those who represent this truth. And as the truth becomes all the more clear, it will be resisted all the more fiercely. Saul's violence – 'breathing threats to slaughter the Lord's disciples' (Acts 9:1) – seeks to remove the source of the truth, for this truth is a profound threat to his present identity. On the road to Damascus Saul discovered the truth through his victim, the person whom he was trying to persecute – the Lord. Such was the profundity of the change required, Saul had to learn to 'see' again: a new reality was brought to him through the truth of his victim.

Saul was offered reconciliation by God on the road to Damascus but he was told the truth about what he was doing: 'Saul, Saul, why are you persecuting me?' (v4). He was given an account, the injustice was named. And at the same time this persecutor is received by Christ. He is given a new identity and becomes Paul. He is forgiven not through an act of absolution – no one says to him 'You are free of guilt' – but through being made an apostle to the Gentiles, set apart to suffer for the Lord (vv13-17).

Saul's enmity was not only against God; it was also directed at other human beings, the Christian community. It has both a vertical and a horizontal dimension. Similarly, his reconciliation has both a vertical and a horizontal dimension. The persecutor is received both by the risen Christ and by the community he persecuted. In fact, he becomes a builder of the community he sought to destroy (v20).

Times of change bring new possibilities and new 'truths'. Often they will be fiercely resisted because identities are based on old 'truths'. Violence is a way of driving out new possibilities. The killing of Stephen in Acts seven is one example. And Saul is there, looking after the coats of those carrying out the murder. The Swiss artist Felix Hoffmann has a piece of stain glass in a church in Bern showing the stoning. Saul is on the fringe of the crowd looking on, arms folded, approving the killing, the very picture of a young, fastidious zealot. But, perhaps, the conversion of Saul begins here.

In some situations some people may desperately continue their violence, e.g. through internecine disputes, because they can see no way forward. The desperate violence of the *colons* in Algeria before Independence is one example of a people who saw their world collapsing and who could not find a new possibility.

Reconciliation: A Step Beyond – Acts 10:9-16

Peter is on a housetop in Joppa and falls into a trance and sees:

heaven thrown open and something like a big sheet being let down to earth by its four corners; it contained every possible sort of animal and bird, walking, crawling or flying ones. A voice then said to him, 'Now Peter, kill and eat.' And Peter replies, 'But I have never yet eaten anything profane or unclean' (vv 11-14).

Peter is trapped by his own cultural and ancestral voices. He had his life worked out on the basis of separation and purity and he is challenged by the vision of the sheet at the very foundations of all that he believed was important. Peter discovered that God had already identified with the people on the other side of the wall of separation. God had already taken a step beyond. He had done the unexpected.

The way of reconciliation demands that someone steps out beyond the normal boundaries of human life; it invites a person, or a group, to walk beyond the established frontiers so that something new can happen. The visit of Sadat to Egypt is an example of such an action. The Evangelical Church in Germany's *Memorandum on Eastern European Countries*, published in 1965, paved the way for steps towards reconciliation with Germany's eastern neighbours, even though at the time West German public reaction was largely negative. In 1970 on his visit to the Polish capital, during a ceremony before the ruins of the Warsaw ghetto, Chancellor Willy Brandt, overwhelmed by emotion, fell to his knees. The photograph in the newspapers gave another impetus to the debate in Germany – the two governments continued negotiations and the two peoples became ready for the Treaties of Reconciliation of 1990/91.

The Images of 'Stranger' and 'Alien' – Ephesians 2:12-16[9]
The author of Ephesians uses the images of 'strangers' and 'aliens' for Gentiles in an unreconciled state from God. These images remind us of the principle way human beings choose to draw boundaries that secure their safety and security. They do this by exclusion, placing beyond that boundary those who are not 'us' – the 'others'. They are the aliens and strangers. And it is when people become aliens and strangers that killing can take place, for we are in a world of antagonised division.

Jesus on the Cross exposes the mechanisms of exclusion in which we are all involved and becomes an alien and a stranger. The Greek words translated by 'reconciliation' or 'to reconcile' all derive from *katallage*, 'to exchange', and this in turn is derived from *allos* , meaning 'the other'. The words thus carry with them the sense of exchanging places with the 'other', and therefore being in solidarity with, rather than being over against, the 'other'.

Jesus is the 'go-between' person – who crosses the boundaries and meets the aliens and the strangers. He follows the way of exchange. Jesus on the Cross becomes an alien and a stranger; he dies outside the camp (Heb 13:13). He breaks down the dividing wall of antagonised division and opens communication. The text reminds us of the gigantic costs of this reconciling work –

'through the cross'. The result of the Cross is a drawing together of the human world, an overcoming of hostility: because of the death of Jesus, God and the world are no longer strangers and aliens to each other and thus too the world is not for ever divided into communities of antagonised division that are for ever strange and alien to each other. Instead aliens and strangers become citizens (v19).

Every situation that requires reconciliation needs 'go-between' people who can open up doors of communication and negotiate boundaries. The Quakers John and Diana Lampen played a significant role as 'go-between' people between the security forces and the Republican movement in Londonderry in the 1980s/early 1990s. The relationship between the Redemptorist priest Father Alex Reid and the Leader of Sinn Féin, Gerry Adams, and his 'go-between' role between Adams and a number of key players – including the British and Irish governments – has been shown[10] to be extraordinarily important in the Northern Ireland peace process. Frank Wright taught history to UVF prisoners in Long Kesh in the early 1970s. Gusty Spence, who was leader of the UVF prisoners, said of Frank:

> He was chronically honest and supportive and tried to understand who my men were, what they were doing there, and what their motives were ... we shared many thoughts and explorations ... he had a humanity that we have seldom seen.[11]

'Go-between people' have often had particular experiences that make them particularly able to follow the way of exchange. Ray Davey, founder of the Corrymeela Community, was a prisoner of war and was outside Dresden in February 1945, when the city was fire bombed. This provided the impetus for his subsequent ministry of reconciliation.

CHAPTER FIVE

Churches and Reconciliation

Introduction
Christian faith challenges all exclusive claims of tribe, tradition and political commitment. The gospel invites us into the space created by Christ and to find there those who were previously our enemies. It therefore seeks to break down the enmity between us: enmity caused by different traditions, and national, political and religious loyalties. The gospel opens up for us a view of wholeness, justice and living in right relations which sees the whole world as potential brothers and sisters; a nourishing and fulfilment of the human. This is a vision of a new humanity reconciled in Christ and living together in a new community.

Through Christ a new relationship is established between those who accept the gift of reconciliation: strangers become citizens and aliens are recognised as members of the household of God (Eph 2:19). This redeemed people are called to be a community of reconciliation – a community of openness and inclusion – united round the death and resurrection of Jesus Christ.

At the same time, the reality is that churches are part of communities and nations; they cannot be other. They are chaplains, reflectors, consciences, restrainers, discerners, givers of wisdom, custodians of collective memory and places of community belonging. Churches bring 'their' community before God. They are places where the 'specialness' and stories of communities and nations can be celebrated. Much of this is necessary and good, but there is another side. 'Specialness' can lead to exclusivity and a sense of superiority. Churches can be places where we are told – implicitly and explicitly – who does not belong to our community: by who is prayed for and who is not, by the contents of sermons, and by the symbols displayed or not displayed.

The church is a home for the community or the nation. And

at the same time it lives by a story of a Jesus who died outside the camp (Heb 13:13) and who, while completely a Jew, did not belong to his world (Jn 17:14) and was driven out of it by those who did not want to be disturbed by another way. All our 'homes' – personal, communal, national – are radically de-centred by Jesus: 'For there is no eternal city for us in this life, but we look for one in the life to come' (Heb 13:14). And the church is a community where Jew and Greek, bond and free, belong (1 Cor 12:13); in its very essence it transcends all social, cultural and national boundaries.

The church lives in a tension: in the world, but not of it (cf Jn 18:36). The danger is that in situations of communal conflict the tension collapses and, as the Croation theologian Miroslav Volf says:

> … Churches often find themselves accomplices in war rather than agents of peace. We find it difficult to distance ourselves from our own culture so we echo its reigning opinions and mimic its practices.[1]

The Janus Face of Religion

Religion plays a profoundly ambiguous role in conflict situations. On the one hand, it can encourage hatred; anti-Catholicism is particularly potent in Northern Ireland, and has political consequences. Churches can reinforce community division and harden boundaries; Catholic views and rules on mixed marriage and the importance of church schools have had significant consequences in Northern Irish society. Religion can give divine sanction to nationalisms, political positions and violence. Shimon Peres says of Hezbollah, the Lebanese Shiite terrorist group: 'These are religious people. With the religious you can hardly negotiate. They think they have supreme permission to kill people and go to war. This is their nature.'[2] In conflict situations theologies of enmity, superiority and distorted recognition of others can easily gain prominence, e.g. the Dutch Reformed Church in South Africa theologically legitimated apartheid. When churches and religions find themselves on different sides of a fear-threat relationship between two communities, there can be a political/religious symbiosis, e.g. in Northern Ireland – Protestantism/Unionism, Catholicism/Nationalism.

Churches find it difficult to establish any critical distance from the pressures coming from 'their' community. The temptation is to identify without reserve and to become chaplains to 'their' community. Ian Linden has written[3] about the 'stranglehold that ethnicity had gained' in the church in Rwanda. The church 'had never seriously challenged Hutu or Tutsi identity as potentially open to being re-imagined in a Christian form, because ethnicity had always been taken as a given'. When the genocide occurred in 1994 the church found it very difficult to resist the dynamics of hatred and killing. There were a significant number of prominent Christians involved in the killings (although there were church people who resisted and were martyred). In the former Yugoslavia some churches became guardians of national identity. There was a religious-national symbiosis and some people who committed war crimes regarded themselves as defending not only their nation but their faith as well.

On the other hand, religion can be a force for restraint and this has been generally true in Northern Ireland. Without the churches the situation would have been a lot worse; the preaching and living out of non-retaliation, forbearance and forgiveness has had real social consequences. The churches opposed those who espoused violence and the gods of nationalism. Churches working together have been a force for good; they have helped lessen the religious/political symbiosis. The developing pattern of church leaders and others meeting together over the last thirty years in Northern Ireland, of clergy visiting victims of violence together, has been a significant public witness. Churches have been encouragers to politicians seeking political compromise. There have been many individuals and groups – for example, the Corrymeela Community – working for peace and reconciliation. Contacts were established by church groups with paramilitary organisations; clergy and others acted as go-betweens. The Irish Council of Churches, together with the Roman Catholic Church, have had a peace education programme working in schools, and so on. And, nevertheless, the picture is very mixed and deeply ambiguous. Some black, much grey, a little white. Churches are part of the problem and struggle to be part of the solution.

The church in Fiji illustrates this well. During the coup in

1987 by the military (many of the instigators were deeply steeped in Christian religious practice and openly invoked their faith as a guide for their action)

> the temptation was strong to align the church to the interests of chauvinist politicians who seized control of the State and sought legitimation of their rule that pitched one ethnic community against another. It fell upon another set of church leaders to defy the military and secular authorities in advocating an alternative course of reconciliation.[4]

In the former Yugoslavia, after peace was declared, religious institutions and communities, by and large, found themselves appealing for forgiveness in their general statements but not being able to stop blaming and judging each other.

The problem is that politics appears to dominate the churches more than *vice versa*. This is one very significant factor in inhibiting churches in being agents of co-operation and raises profound questions about what is more important: religious commitment or political commitment. In theological terms, we are talking about the issue of idolatry.

Churches tend to reflect people's fears, reflect community divisions, reflect a community experience of violence and threat, rather than act as agents of change or transformers of conflict. Thus the Protestant Churches in Northern Ireland often talk about law and order, reflecting a community under siege, and the Catholic Church often talks about justice, reflecting a community feeling of victimisation. Churches not only reflect people's fears; they can also amplify them (witness the role of the Rev Dr Ian Paisley in Northern Ireland).

Local churches, in particular, often reflect people's sense of fear and threat. They are places of ordered calm – a safe space – where we are among our own; our enemies are outside. They are 'protective fortresses for threatened people'[5] in the words of the political scientist Duncan Morrow, speaking of some Protestant churches in Northern Ireland. Or they may be places that assume a symbiosis between religion and national identity, e.g. Catholicism and Irishness. The prayers, the liturgy, the sermons, plaques and flags can tell us who is outside and inside of our concern, who our enemies are, what state we belong to, often in highly oblique and coded ways. And, of course, in some settings a local church may also contain a lot of political difference within it. Then the rule is these differences are never talked about, but we all know they are there. And because never talked about, they can never be dealt with. Clergy in such contexts find themselves in a very unfree and very vulnerable position.

In divided societies fear, anxiety and a sense of threat are encoded; they almost become part of people's genetic make-up. As the dynamics of conflict gather force, individuals and groups disappear into a vortex of antagonism. They are magnetised by violence. It takes very strong people to stand out when all around succumb. And it is true that some people can stand outside the vortex of antagonism. In Northern Ireland some church people are the most committed in terms of peace and reconciliation, common witness and co-operation and have been so since the start of the 'Troubles'. In Rwanda, some Christians were martyred for standing against the ethnic hatred and killing. In Fiji some Christian leaders resisted the coup and stood for reconciliation between ethnic groups.

Transcendent Faith

The church is a witness to the Kingdom of God and the presence of transcendence, and is called to be a community of reconciliation and as such offer a 'space' in the world for those who believe that human society can, if only in anticipation,

> overcome its violent origins, its continuing resentments and mistrust and come to realise its true calling to become the beloved community envisaged in the biblical story.[6]

Thus the church exists that we may know what humanity might be, that is people who are 'different' and 'strange':

- able to stand out against community hatred;
- able to cross community boundaries;
- able to be peacemakers;
- able to be healers;
- able to forgive;
- able to stand with the victims; and
- able to engage in costly action.

When we see this 'difference' and 'strangeness' we are in the presence of transcendence[7] and in the presence of witness to the Kingdom of God. The message of reconciliation is made visible.

As I have said earlier, I am a member of a community of reconciliation, the Corrymeela Community. Corrymeela has worked, often residentially, with a huge mixture of people from all sorts of different backgrounds. We have been journeying together for almost forty years and there are 'graduates' of Corrymeela all over the place. During that time we have learnt the importance of:

- belonging together in a community of diversity;
- reconciliation being a practice, and a journey, not a theory or a strategy or a technique;
- a safe space where people can come and meet each other, where there is an atmosphere of trust and acceptance and where differences can be acknowledged, explored and accepted;
- presence and accompaniment – people who can give time and attention;
- a community of faith being able to bring healing, and so being a 'touching place';
- encounter and relationships; it is only in encounter and relationships that words like trust, reconciliation and forgiveness become real ;
- acknowledging and sharing vulnerability;
- people telling their stories and listening to other peoples' stories. Our identities and lives are based strongly on the stories we tell about ourselves, our families, our communities, our countries. Thus we need places where memories are explored and untangled;
- not writing people off as incorrigible 'baddies' no matter what they have done – this is not to trivialise evil or say wrong does not matter;
- the avoidance of self-righteousness and an awareness of our own hypocrisy;
- surprise and the unexpected; reconciliation is something given as well as a practice;
- taking small steps;
- being sustained and nourished by hope and a vision of a different future;
- being involved for the long haul; and
- a recognition that the transformation of the world is linked to the transformation of ourselves.

The Cornerstone Community, based beside the peace-line in West Belfast, also illustrates what a community of reconciliation can be – at 'the place of intersection':

When the Cornerstone Community came into being twenty years ago, the choice of place to live was deliberate. The house is at the intersection of two communities in West Belfast, two communities then at war. Violence was rampant, people lived with grief, pain, fear and mistrust. A wall was being built to keep us apart. Cornerstone hoped to show there was another way of living. For the place of intersection is also the meeting point, and the function of a cornerstone is to unite the two intersecting parts, making both one (cf Eph 2:20-22).

Twenty years on, we are still at the point of intersection. The physical wall is higher, but many encounters have taken place at the meeting point. We celebrate the fact that the Community house has been a place of welcome where people have met across many divides. We celebrate the way our own lives have been enriched by encounters with visitors from across the world, each one a gift. We celebrate the generosity of the many volunteers who have come to us over the years, bringing their gifts of energy, enthusiasm, caring, practical faith. We celebrate republican ex-prisoners meeting with groups of English church people and tackling difficult questions together, and we celebrate people from different political persuasions using the house as a place to thrash out new political possibilities as part of the peace process. Above all, we celebrate our belief that Jesus Christ is himself the cornerstone.[8]

The Community of Sant' Egidio is a Christian community based in Rome. Comprised of lay Catholics, many of whom also pursue professional careers, the community was formed in the late 1960s to pursue an ecumenical vocation of reconciliation both within the church and in society. Located in the old Carmelite monastery of Sant' Egidio in the Trasteverre quarter of the city, traditionally the home to those on the periphery of Roman society, the community meets daily for worship, for meals and for planning its projects. Members of the community played a vital role over two years in helping to bring the civil war in Mozambique to an end. They have also been involved in many other conflict situations (Albania, Burundi, Kosovo, Guatemala, Algeria and the Democratic Republic of the Congo). A faith community or institution like the Community of Sant' Egidio, can provide a space for the exploration of political alternatives and a setting in which the parties can talk directly to each other, all of this in the context of a consistent and reliable web of human relations which is providing accompaniment and support.

In South Africa a number of churches and congregations played a significant role in the struggle against apartheid, in the transition to full democracy, and in the task of national reconciliation and transformation.[9]

But the reality is that churches in conflict situations have rarely been communities of reconciliation. Thus the profound need for *metanoia*. Spiritual renewal and engaging in the ministry of reconciliation are linked.

Repentance

In speaking to the churches in Northern Ireland, *Sectarianism: A Discussion Document* (1993) said:

What has happened in Northern Irish society calls us to a profound change of heart (*metanoia*). The call is to face reality, to abandon our myths, to accept our part of the responsibility for what has happened and find new ways forward together.[10]

Churches need to remember and feel the pain of failure, to face the damage that has arisen from an unhappy past. They need the grace to turn away from the captivity to political causes and of allowing stories of nationalism and cultural and political identity to overpower the story of the gospel. They need to repent and, in order to make this repentance in a truthful and credible way, churches must also come face to face with the painful reality of their own complicity with, and participation in, the brokenness and fallenness around them.

As people turn to God in repentance, they find that to turn to God is also to turn to one another. And in this, apologies and expressions of regret are important. Some instances of this in Ireland are the following:

• the Catholic Bishop of Ferns, Brendan Comiskey, in June 1998 expressing 'deep sorrow' and asking forgiveness for the

Catholic boycott of Protestant businesses in Fethard-on-Sea, Co Wicklow in 1957;

- the Catholic Bishop of Killaloe, Willie Walsh, in 1997 apologising and asking forgiveness for the 'pain and hurt' caused 'to our non-Roman brethren' by the *Ne Temere* decree, followed by the regret expressed by the Archbishop of Armagh, Sean Brady, on the same subject in the following year;
- the Presbyterian General Assembly passing a resolution in 1966 urging its members 'humbly and frankly to acknowledge and to ask for forgiveness for any attitudes and actions towards our Roman Catholic fellow-countrymen which have been unworthy of our calling as followers of Jesus Christ';
- a representative group of Orange Order chaplains expressing 'deep sorrow' to the Roman Catholic community in Northern Ireland that so many of them had been intimidated out of their houses and that several of their churches had been burnt, after widespread disturbances in early July 1998 connected with the refusal to let an Orange procession go down a road at Drumcree, Co Armagh.

In South Africa the Truth and Reconciliation Commission hearing devoted to the 'Faith Communities' was in some respect an act of confession by the churches. In their submissions all the 'mainline' churches in South Africa acknowledged that they had not done as much as they should have to combat apartheid.

Church leaders confessed that too many of their members had connived with apartheid, and some had been amongst those who had perpetrated atrocious crimes. Hence a major emphasis in their statements was that of penitence for past failure, and a commitment to work for national reconciliation and justice in the future.[11]

The Stuttgart Confession of Guilt in 1945 recognised the Evangelical Church in Germany's share of the responsibility for the terrible things done during the Third Reich. It paved the way for an honest approach to what had happened and for that church's re-entry into the ecumenical community. Pope John Paul II in March 2000 apologised to and asked forgiveness from, a whole series of groups, including the Jews, Gypsies and native peoples.

Bound together with a nation or community, and in a solidarity of sin with the nation or community, such confessions by churches may have a representative or vicarious nature.

Over-identification

Churches and religious communities find themselves over-identified with their 'own' community – the religious / political symbiosis talked about earlier is one aspect of this. The challenge is to find a healthier relationship which involves a capacity for criticism and telling people what they do not want to hear, as well as a capacity to cherish and understand. As Archbishop Rowan Williams said in his enthronement sermon: 'The church has to warn and to lament as well as to comfort.' Bound up with an over-identification is a fear of losing out in a new situation – of losing power, influence, position, identity and security. Thus there is a profound ambivalence about letting go of the old and journeying with all the risks into a new society (the people of Israel discovered that journeying to a Promised Land required years in the wilderness). For journeying into a new society involves being remade.

Relationships

'It's relationships, stupid' – to misquote former President Clinton.

Joseph Liechty and Cecelia Clegg in their book, *Moving Beyond Sectarianism: Religion, Conflict and Reconciliation in Northern Ireland*, write about moving away from a hermeneutic

of negative engagement with others, within their own church tradition, in other Christian traditions and in society, towards a hermeneutic of positive engagement with those who are different, or who are antagonistic. It is a movement away from the type of separation that augments ignorance, fear, and division to the type of engagement that brings the wisdom and the challenge of Christian discipleship to bear on differences within a tradition, differences between traditions, and on the deliberations of society.[12]

In making a positive contribution to a society marked by antagonised division

the Christian churches and faith communities could and would have a significant role in encouraging and assisting people to renew and transform their ways of relating. This is a core strategy of peacebuilding …[13]

And that would also involve working at transforming relationships between themselves. Transforming relationships,
however, needs to occur both institutionally and personally.
Thus there is a ministry of friendship and hospitality which is of
vital significance. All of this should be seen as accepting 'the biblical imperative to engage in prophetic boundary-crossing activities and to be peacemakers.'[14] It is not about abandoning religious truth claims or fidelity to a tradition. What it does do is
place truth and fidelity in the context of relationships and peace.
Differences are faced in honest conversation.

Leadership

Gregory Baum, in the book that he and Harold Wells edited of
accounts of church involvement in reconciliation work, highlights the importance of leadership:

> In all the accounts, reconciliation between groups or peoples
> is promoted by a few Christians with strong convictions sur-
> rounded by many who remain indifferent or are even hostile
> to the idea ... Since reconciliation calls for conversion, the
> leaders exercise a prophetic ministry: they mediate God's
> Word to a reluctant community. Their effort becomes suc-
> cessful only as an increasing number of people enter into the
> new spirit and offer their support for the movement of recon-
> ciliation.[15]

Leadership articulates a vision and encourages and gives permission to the ministry of reconciliation. In Fiji the Catholic
Archbishop of Suva was active in supporting the social movement opposed to the 1987 coup. He encouraged Catholics to
carry out interfaith encounters in each parish to allow indigenous Fijians and Indo-Fijians to share their experiences during
the coup, learn of each other's sufferings and frustrations and
nurture hope for the future. Thus healing fora were created
where people could hear and be heard.

The Ritual Action and Practice of the Faith Community

One of the things that the faith community has most to offer is its
ritual actions and practices, i.e. in liturgy. As the English theologian Keith Clements says:

> Liturgy is about how we incarnate in drama and symbol our

transformation by grace: the transformation from defeat to victory, from bondage to freedom, from guilt to forgiveness, from conflict to reconciliation, from death to life.[16]

Liturgy should give us an anticipation of the final reconciliation: The Lord's supper, the Eucharist, is a foretaste of the great feast when people shall come from east and west, north and south, and sit down together in the kingdom of God.[17]

However, an authentic liturgy for reconciliation also

needs to enable us to express the truth of our present conflicts, the hurt and the anger and the bitter desire for vengeance, as in the Psalms: these have to be brought out into the open and offered to God, who knows how to deal with them all.[18]

In Conclusion

Jesus calls people to go with him on a journey of risk and encounter. Christians are to have confidence in the gospel and in the power of Christ to transform relationships. The story of Jesus walking over the water (Mt 14:28-32) is saying that his faithful followers will not be swamped by chaos (water is an image of chaos here), and that, even doubting, they can be safe when they cling to him. Therefore, a task for the churches and for Christians in conflict situations is to help prepare people for change, to hold people in making transitions and to encourage them to live confidently, to enter into relationships and to create communities which allow for and enhance the freedom of others. At their centre, churches have a narrative of forgiveness, reconciliation, new possibilities and new identities which, if it was really believed and acted on, could be transforming.

CHAPTER SIX

Dealing with the Past

Introduction

How people remember profoundly affects how they behave in the present, and significantly affects their politics; thus in Northern Ireland the politics of historic grievance and the politics of siege. Our accumulated history is part of today's reality. It pushes people back to standing by their 'own' and against their enemies. Unhealed memories can enslave and condemn us to a seemingly endless living out of the past. Grasped by the ghosts of the past we are unable to imagine a different future. It is therefore important to understand how memory operates.

MEMORY

The Importance of Memory

Nations and peoples weave their sense of themselves into narratives. These (foundational) stories tell us what we need to know about ourselves and how we remember what has happened to us. The stories function not only in maintaining community identity and solidarity, but also in shaping the relationship of the group with others. And the stories, in turn, are shaped by these relationships.

America, in part, owes its national identity to the prevalence of powerful stories which arose out of its early history. Many are attached to founding 'fathers', others to the experience of nation building. Perhaps the most powerful story is that which developed out of the frontier experience of an emerging nation. Manifest destiny is how historians label it, the belief that the settlement and taming of this vast largely uninhabited land by European colonialists was a divinely destined event. The story goes as follows: a brave pioneering people, escaping from religious and political oppression in Europe, meet great obstacles in realising their dreams of a free land for free people in an untamed wilderness. Among these obstacles are 'savage' natives who use terrorist tactics to attempt to thwart their designs. With God's help the brave settlers defeat the 'savages' and force them off the land, at least the best land, thus making way for those who are better able to exploit the God-given resources that it yields. This story continues to shape American self-identity, as evidenced in the ease with which politicians, most recently President George Bush, are able to rally support for foreign policy ventures drawing on key elements of this myth ('any attack on America is an attack on freedom').

The symbolic narratives of groups are incorporated in flags,[1] anthems, songs, speeches, national holidays and war memorials. They are also incorporated into festivals and rituals, e.g. Remembrance Day and the Twelfth of July.

Whatever is remembered has a direct bearing on the things that preoccupy us today. Thus remembering is always selective. Remembering and forgetting are two intertwined ways of reconstructing the past, and thereby giving identity. All groups depend on the forgetting of events and of people that do not fit into the 'story'.

No memory tells us simply what is the case because every remembrance is laden with individual and collective desires and interests, as well as collectively shared convictions – which are themselves shaped by 'cultural memory'. Thus, for instance, arguments about how many Serbs were killed in Croatian concentration camps during the Second World War, or the number of Protestants killed in 1641, are not just about facts. Facts and events need larger narratives, and since larger narratives are in dispute, facts and events are in dispute too. There are different 'memories' of the same event.

People often construct their past using a particular interpretative 'key'. This is a way of reading history, enabling people to understand themselves, but also how their enemies fit into the story. One example are the Serbs: in 1389 they fought against the emergent Ottoman Empire at the Battle of Kosovo Polje and lost. Remembering this battle came to be the interpretative 'key' for how the Serb people understood themselves. The Yugoslav dissident Milovan Djilas said: 'Wipe away Kosovo from the Serb mind and soul and we are no more.'[2] The Serbs became perennial mourners. They had fought to defend the values of Christian Europe. However, Christian Europe, and particularly their Catholic neighbours, never appreciated the sacrifice, and the Serbs came to see themselves as heroic victims. President Slobodan Milosevic sought to draw on the story at the 600th anniversary in 1989 to reassert his own power and proclaimed 'never again would Islam subjugate the Serbs'.[3] He began a process that led the Serb nation to disaster and more trauma.

Jewish identity has been built round the trauma of events, in particular in the twentieth century the holocaust. The novelist David Grossman has commented that there is no week in the Israeli calendar in which there is not a memorial day of some sort for a traumatic event.

What Interpretative Keys Are Used in Irish Memory?
1. The Ulster Protestant Community
What interpretative keys are used to construct Ulster Protestant memory and identity? There are identity stories of:
  Siege (1689, siege of Derry);
  Massacre at the hands of Catholics (1641);
  Resistance (1689, 1912 Home Rule, 1985 Anglo-Irish Agreement);
  Covenanting together (1912);
  Blood sacrifice (1641, 1690 Battle of the Boyne, 1916 Battle of the Somme);
  Struggle and deliverance (1689, 1690);
  Victory over Catholics (1690).
Thus, the Protestant story is a saga of conquest, endurance, sacrifice, deliverance, fear of betrayal, and the endless need for vigilance. The hope is that the people will continue to escape and have the victory. Memory is a form of resistance. The story is endlessly replayed: the parades are a mnemonic device, a ritual recalling of the need for vigilance. Important in this is the religious dimension. There is a sacred story of Protestant martyrdom and Catholic duplicity. There is an identification with the history of Israel in the Old Testament: the story of the covenant community – a chosen people – who have been delivered but are surrounded by pagan enemies liable to corrupt with their idolatry and destroy with their violence.

2. The Irish Catholic Community

What interpretative keys are used to construct Irish Catholic memory and identity? There are identity stories of:

Defeat (Battle of Kinsale 1603, 1690);

Victimisation (Cromwell, the Famine, Partition);

Betrayal (Treaty of Limerick 1691);

Dispossession of the land (17th Century);

Injustice and oppression (18th Century Penal Laws);

The eternal cycle of sacrificial martyrdom and rebirth/redemption (1916).

Some of this is linked to the sacrificial themes of Irish Catholicism (Calvary, blood and redemption) and stories of endurance in the faith during times of persecution. Memory is also a form of resistance in the Catholic tradition and there are rituals that sustain the resistance (e.g. the annual orations at the Republican plots on Easter Sunday).

3. What the Traditions Share

Sacrifice and victimisation are important interpretative keys in the way that the past is understood in both traditions. The heroic sacrifices of the past require continuing honour, respect and loyalty.

Memory and Power

Victory gives the victor the right to render the 'official' story. They can tell a story of triumphalism and superiority, of manifest destiny, of a mission to civilise, depending on the chosen interpretative 'key' or 'keys'. The 'nasty' bits – often a reality of massacre and murder – can be forgotten.

The vanquished retain their memories – what one has suffered one never forgets – and out of them narrate their own version of what happened. The story becomes a story of resistance, a resentment of that defeat, and a hope for a decisive transformation of the situation.

The vanquished often have to fight the version of events, the story, as told by the dominant people or colonial power. David James and Jillian Wychel illustrate this from the experience of the Maoris in Aotearoa/New Zealand (the power to name is also part of the struggle between rival stories):

... it has been difficult for the Maori story even to be heard, let alone accepted, by the majority. The Pakeha community [the majority community] and the monocultural state in Aotearoa/New Zealand have until recently held an almost complete grip on the education system and the media, and therefore on easily accessible information.

One of the peripheral but strongly held themes of the Pakeha story is of the assimilation of the Maori to the new national order introduced by the Crown. One of the central themes of the Maori story is of resistance to assimilation despite all attempts by the Crown and the dominant culture and of continual demands for local self-determination and for a voice in national matters.

The occupation of Pakaitore/Moutoa Gardens in 1995 was a classic instance of the difference between the two stories. For most citizens, relying on the mainstream media for their information, it was a story of a turbulent time of youthful anger and violence, of gang involvement, of vandalism against historic monuments, and of the final vindication of the law through the court declaration that ownership of the land did properly lie with the local council.

For the occupiers, the story was one of mainly disciplined protest against the delay and denial of justice, of withstanding harassment from the police and the community, and of the drawing together of the iwi, young and old, into a twelve-week intensive seminar-cum-political negotiation which has helped to create new representative bodies for the iwi ... The legal title to the land was never the main issue.[4]

Often the oppressed internalise the oppressor and their story. Even after liberation or a change of circumstances, the story can live on in the minds of the former oppressed. Envy, resentment and enmity can continue to be present. The vanquished often have to face the forgetfulness of the victor. The Irish have a story about the killing instigated by Oliver Cromwell at Drogheda in 1649; it is important to their identity. The English have no story at all.

The vanquished often tell their stories in ways that demonise the conqueror: they refuse to recognise their humanity and see them as incapable of changing. Memory can be a form of thirst for vengeance. And the victims find it difficult to acknowledge that they can be perpetrators too. As the *Irish Times* columnist Fintan O'Toole says of the Irish: 'In our collective memory we are always the victims, never the perpetrators.'[5]

The victor can attempt to erase the memory of those who have suffered. Thus, ethnic cleansing is an attempt to eradicate the accusing truth of the past. As Michael Ignatieff says:

> In its wake the past may be rewritten so that no record of the victim's presence is allowed to remain. Victory encloses the victim in a forgetting that removes the very possibility of guilt, shame or remorse, the emotions required for a sustained encounter with the truth.[6]

Memory and Forgetting in a Contested Space

Before antagonism intensified in the nineteenth century, people in Northern Ireland experienced the world in ways that reflected 'Protestant' and 'Catholic' much less sharply than was the case later. In this, they paralleled many societies in Eastern Europe at the same time. For instance, Albanians and Serbs lived relatively peacefully side by side in Kosovo before and during the Ottoman Empire. Ethnic tensions only began to increase in the nineteenth century, with the rise of Serb nationalism.

However, as rivalry increases – often under the impact of the rise of nationalism – communities of fear and threat often emerge. Identities that once were permeable begin to be closed off. Differences are emphasised. As fears increased, people began to focus on the moments of antagonism in the past, e.g. stories of massacre. Remembrance of earlier events only grew in strength as contestation increased. For instance, the first commemoration of the Battle of the Boyne took place one hundred years after the event and most of the famous ballads about 1798 were written not in the immediate aftermath of the rebellion but in preparation for the centenary celebrations.

Antagonism controls memory. Memory tells us who our enemies are today and what they have done to us in the past, or what they have been stopped from doing in the past. History is gradually shaped into an 'us' and 'them'. Parallel stories develop.

David James and Jillian Wychel have illustrated this from their experience of visiting the Tower Museum in Londonderry:

> The concept of parallel stories arising out of a contested space was dramatically illustrated in one part of the Tower Museum in L'Derry. A corridor ran between windowed displays on either side. On one side was the Nationalist story of specific events, told through its symbols and artefacts, and on the other side the Unionist story of the same events. On the one side the kerbstones that linked the corridor were painted orange, white and green; on the other red, white and blue.[7]

Antagonists tell parallel stories, but antagonists are also interlocked. Thus, there is an interdependence of memory. The theologian Alan Falconer says of Northern Ireland: 'The identity of each community has been shaped by the actions, attitudes and declarations of other communities.'[8] We have shaped each other, including each other's memories.

Antagonism simplifies the story, controls what is remembered and tends to exonerate us from what happens in the conflict. We simply cannot see our role in the 'play': that we are caught in a fear-threat relationship.

As antagonism progresses, scapegoating and demonisation intensify. People normally belong to different but overlapping identities: religious, cultural, ethnic, national. In situations of conflict, these identities tend to fuse. Thus, for instance, a religious threat becomes a political threat, and *vice versa*.

As antagonism escalates, all we can remember are the threats to our community and ourselves. The 'hopeful' bits – the stories of good relationships and co-operation – drop out of history because they are seen as unimportant in the light of subsequent events. Frank Wright has illustrated this[9] in his retelling of a forgotten 'moment' of co-operation between Protestant and Catholic in the Tenant League's struggle to protect the position of tenants in mid-nineteenth century Ulster. Wright has also demonstrated that the on-going division between Protestant and Catholic has been shaped by the presence of Britain. Both sides remember how this presence has affected them; the British do not remember – it is not important for their identity.

The Suppression of Memory

What we remember is a socially constructed narrative, an unwritten agreement about what is publicly remembered and acknowledged. These constructed narratives drive out part of reality, the bits that do not fit into the narrative. Thus, the Pope's support for King William in 1690, and the Presbyterian United Irishmen disappear from Ulster Protestant remembrance. The many Irish Catholic Nationalists who died in the First World War did not fit into the new national myth with its authorised memories. They disappeared into an historical limbo.

A 'deep remembering' (Geiko Mueller–Fahrenholtz) will disclose a complexity of events and a complexity of identity. If we cannot tolerate a complex image of ourselves, e.g. admitting elements of shame and elements of guilt, then we distort ourselves and we distort our neighbour. There is the danger of demonisation and scapegoating, and we risk feelings of rage, frustration, self-hatred and self-pity. A community in its rage and despair from loss of power can retreat inwards, see itself as the victim and refuse to examine the past. Particular memories are preserved as the community closes itself off.

Memories may be suppressed because to talk about them is too painful. The history of our guilt may be hidden, remembrance blocked by denial, discomfort and defensiveness (the willed amnesia of the perpetrator or victor). The victims may be reduced to silence or unable to speak.[10] Returning to the point of pain has great difficulty for both victims and perpetrators. But if deeds are not identified and named they maintain their hidden power.

The unacknowledged and sub-conscious pains of older generations can have a contaminating impact on the younger ones. Not only the sins of the fathers but the pains of hurt and shame may be passed down the generations.

The danger of suppressing the past is a theme which snakes its way through many of the books of the Jewish writer, Elie Wiesel. In his novel *The Fifth Son* the father, who was a concentration camp survivor, feels unable to talk about the past to the son. The effect was that the past could not become really past; it continued hopelessly to entangle the present, and in particular the life of the son. The book ends with the son saying:

A sad summing up: I have moved heaven and earth. I have risked damnation and madness by interrogating the memories of the living and the dreams of the dead in order to live the life of those who, near and far, continue to haunt me: but when, yes when, shall I finally begin to live my life, my own?[11]

Similarly, Seamus Deane, in his novel *Reading in the Dark*, tells the story of acts of betrayal which took place in Derry in the 1920s. They profoundly affect one family but they could never be openly talked about. The lost uncle hovers over the family and the family house is 'as cunning and articulate as a labyrinth, closely designed with someone sobbing at the heart of it'.[12]

We may not be able to talk honestly about what happened. The Irish historian Tom Garvin speaks about what happened after the Irish Civil War:

... for a long time after the end of the Civil War, a lot of people didn't like talking about it, a sort of conspiracy was entered into by a lot of people – to ensure that the bitterness of the Irish Civil War was not transmitted to a younger and possibly more innocent generation.[13]

The comments of Terence McCaughey should also be noted:

However, there is another side to the story. The silence did not in fact subdue the resentment; the fact that wounds are not spoken of does not ensure that they do not suppurate. And it is plausibly arguable that Irish political discourse was stultified for two generations, and that imaginative political action on the question of Northern Ireland was inhibited by the fear of speaking too much or too openly about what had happened in the earlier years of the century.[14]

The construction of a state, the re-building of society, the need to work with former opponents, the compromises that an end to conflict require, a realisation that no-one has clean hands, fear of stirring up new bitterness, fears about the amount of truth that can be borne, the psychological burden on individuals, a wish that future generations do not bear similar anguish: some or all of these things may seem to require a prudent silence or a determination to let bygones be bygones.

It may well be that this approach may 'work'. A generation may 'background' its hurt, pain and bitterness and carry them to the grave in order to avoid passing them on to a younger generation. The flow of memory may be turned off; the story not passed on. And thus a conflict may be laid to rest, the wounds healed over, reconciliation achieved by time and forgetting. For instance, some countries – France after the Second World War, Spain after Franco, and Poland under its first post-Solidarity government – sought to draw a 'thick line' under the past. In Mozambique the conviction was that 'the less we dwell on the past, the more likely reconciliation will be.'[15]

This solution – ultimately a wager that peace and stability and getting along with people do not require telling the truth about the past – may be available in particular situations, although it should be made clear that particular people and groups have carried the burden of making it 'work', e.g. victims. In other situations, the danger may be that if the demons of the past are not faced the pragmatic and necessary agreements made will be of a precarious nature. There will be a constant danger of them breaking down and of the past repeating itself. Dangerous silences may be created which can break into the bitter voice of mutual recrimination, with the risk of setting off a new round of the cycle of conflict. Thus, the 'thick line' under the past approach has its dangers. By repressing the real history of the interethnic carnage between 1941 and 1945 in the former Yugoslavia, the Titoist regime helped to create the conditions for its return.

There must also be a question whether a 'thick line' under the past approach is even possible today. In Spain the past is being literally dug up as the mass graves of those murdered by Franco's execution squads are disinterred. Villages are having to confront painful issues of internecine conflicts because the Left was also involved in atrocities. And all the range of feelings emerge. In one village[16] one woman says: 'I can never forget what they did. The killers were all from the village. But I can pardon them. If we don't do that, we end up being as bad as they are.' Another man says that younger generations have found it easier to bury the ancient enmities. Some members of the traditional rightwing families in the village had quietly expressed their regrets about the murder of his grandmother. For others in the village the tales of horror, despite the decades, produce rage. Another man, who drove his cart in the middle of the night to pick up bodies of local republicans who had been shot, is dubious of delving into the past. 'If you stir up shit, the stink rises,' he says. However, the past will return whether we want it or not.

The Dangerous Power of Memory

The American Eastern Orthodox theologian Stanley Harakas makes it very clear that there is a dangerous power of memory which can 'overpower' the present, even in people who think they are immune from prejudice:

> Those who seek to foster reconciliation must understand that they are dealing with deep, ingrained, and complex memories, identities, hurts, and suffering. Often these memories become so dominant that they provide powerful reasons for maintaining divisions and antipathies long after they have taken place. Taking lives of their own, they colour emotions, attitudes, and judgements. I am a first-generation Greek American. The bitterness of four hundred years of second class citizenship of my people under Ottoman rule is etched into my psyche. I remember stories told by my father, rejoicing at the expulsion of Turkish armed forces from his home island of Samos in the Aegean Sea. A few years ago, I was seeking to purchase a home. A real estate dealer showed me a home owned by Turkish Americans, decorated to reflect their homeland. I, who thought I was immune to prejudice, found myself agitated and unwilling to consider the home for purchase![17]

Commemoration of past events is frequently a pitched battle between opposing ideologies and groups. The past is an argument about the present. Often commemoration tells more about contemporary needs than about the events themselves. The literary critic Edna Longley says: 'Commemorations are as selective as sympathies. They honour our dead, not your dead.'[18]

Commemoration can revive conflict. The ritual setting of commemorations can trigger historic enmities like nothing else. Sir Kenneth Bloomfield, the Victims' Commissioner for Northern Ireland, in his report *We Will Remember Them*, speaks of 'the first stirrings of the current conflict in the clash of conflicting ideologies in 1966, at the time of commemoration of the Easter Rising and the Battle of the Somme respectively'.[19] It is no accident that these are the two defining events in modern Irish history and that they have been told as stories of heroic suffering and sacrifice. The 600th anniversary of the Battle of Kosovo Polje was used to spark off a new round of conflict in the former Yugoslavia.

Memorials often tend to perpetuate the past and its hurt. Jane Leonard, in a report entitled *Memorials* (1997), says that some of the memorials to those killed in the 'Troubles' reflect:

experiences of loss, desires for revenge, national and religious identity, bewilderment and continuing vulnerability ...[20]

This suggests the difficulty of common remembrance in a context of a civil conflict where victims (and their families) were often bitterly opposed to each other. There is still no common memorial to the dead of the Civil War in the South of Ireland.

There is a dangerous power of memory to stir up hatred and desire for revenge. This is because in places like Rwanda, the former Yugoslavia, and Ireland, the past continues to torment because it is not really past. The past 'contaminates' the present. There is no saving distance between past and present.

Such societies are not living in a serial order of time but in a simultaneous one. The German theologian Geiko Mueller-Fahrenholz tells a story of a visit to the Republic in 1969:

Somewhere south of Dublin we passed a village and the remains of what would have been a large mediaeval church caught our eye. So we stopped and walked over to the ruins. On our way back to the car, we met a peasant woman. Pointing with her thumb to the ruined church she said grimly: 'Cromwell did that to us'.[21]

This story can be paralleled by the explanation given by a Belfast woman to a member of the Faith and Politics Group why Orangemen are not allowed to attend Catholic services: 'It's because of all those people they killed' – the killing she was referring to was the massacre of Protestants in 1641.

For the women, yesterday and today were the same. Michael Ignatieff says about the Balkans:

Simultaneity, it would seem, is the dreamtime of revenge. Crimes can never be safely fixed in the historical past; they remain locked in the eternal present, crying out for blood.[22]

Insisting on the importance of remembering the past is not enough. We need to remember well, recognising that in remembrance lies the possibility of both vengeance and reconciliation.

Positive Recovery of Memory
Memories can be recovered without the renewal of bitterness. We can begin to face the complexity and the pain. The following are two examples:

The first is an extract from a letter which appeared in *The Irish Times* of 11 December 1997 from Una O'Higgins O'Malley, whose father was Kevin O'Higgins, the Irish Free State's Minister for Justice and External Affairs and who was murdered in 1927. It concerns remembrance of the Irish Civil War:

> Your columnist Vincent Browne can be a formidable confronter on radio but, on reflection, I found something important in his recent accusation to Nora Owen TD that Fine Gael, while priding itself on its part in founding this State, had never openly expressed sorrow for the 77 executions and for such incidents as Ballyseedy carried out in the name of its predecessor, Cumann na nGael. I utterly refute, however, his facile taunts that Cumann na nGael paid no price for all of this. For a start, they lost Michael Collins and I think, among other things, of the assassination of their Vice-President and of his father (my father and grandfather). But this letter is not about 'what-aboutery'; rather it is an attempt to suggest the necessity for some structured way of together remembering, expressing sorrow for, and maybe even repenting of, the violence of our shared past.
>
> I have difficulty with this word 'repenting' it is because I don't see how succeeding generations can really take responsibility for what was done before their time in circumstances with which they are not familiar. However, insofar as we have overlooked the anguish of the other side and failed to attempt reconciliation with them, we do have matters of which to repent.
>
> Some years ago the leaders of Ógra Fianna Fáil and of Young Fine Gael (grandsons of Sean Lemass and of Kevin O'Higgins respectively) together laid a wreath of shamrocks at the Four Courts in shared remembrance of all who had lost

their lives as a result of the Civil War – part of a Walk of Remembrance organised by the Glencree Centre for Reconciliation. At that time, it would not have been possible to have had participation from Sinn Féin. But at a concele-brated Mass in Booterstown on the 60th anniversary of the assassination of O'Higgins, he was remembered in the com-pany of the three Republicans who had killed him – some-thing which brought great peace to at least two of the families involved.

The second is a report from *The Irish Times* of 25 November 1997 of the promotion of joint remembrance of the Irish dead of the First World War:

The government is to contribute £150,000 towards the pur-chase of a Peace Park and the construction of a Round Tower in Messines Ridge, West Flanders, to commemorate the 50,000 Irishmen from both sides of the Border who died in the First World War in the 300-mile battlefield in France and Belgium.

The Taoiseach, Mr Ahern, said yesterday this would serve as 'a powerful symbol of reconciliation'.

The project is being carried out by the organisation, A Journey of Reconciliation, whose joint executive chairmen are former Fine Gael Donegal TD, Mr Paddy Harte and Mr Glen Barr, former senior political spokesman of the Ulster Defence Association.

Mr Ahern said, 'I thought it was an excellent idea and I was glad to recommend it to the government for financial support.' He wanted to commend the people who had un-dertaken the project.

Today both patrons and trustees of the Journey of Reconciliation will travel to Messines to meet the Burgo-meister, Mr Jean Liefooghe, and an inter-denominational cer-emony will take place which will celebrate the turning of the sod on the proposed site of the war memorial.

As a memorial, it will recognise the savagery of war, and the futility and the inhuman scale of the killing.

It will also become a place where both communities can join together in remembrance. Its construction will involve young Protestants and Catholics from north and south. In addition, voluntary contributions and assistance from the business community on both sides of the Border will be vital to the project.

The design of the Peace Park and the Round Tower symbolises the ideas and features representative of the entire island of Ireland. Four areas characteristic of the provinces will be treated in landscape terms.

The Round Tower was chosen as it predates the Reformation and political divisions in Ireland. No one political or religious party can lay claim over it. The symbol of ancient Ireland, Newgrange, is relocated in the design so the position of the sun will shine down the site axis and enter an opening in the Tower at 11 am on November 11th, which was the exact hour and date of the Armistice in 1918.

In 2002 a leading figure from Sinn Féin, Tom Hartley, and a leading figure from one of the Loyalist political parties, David Ervine, were able to visit the battlefield of the Somme together and make a television programme about it. The Irish people who died in the First World War have been able to be remembered ecumenically in a service in St Anne's Cathedral, Belfast, in April 2003 which included the Sinn Féin Lord Mayor, Alex Maskey, other Sinn Féin politicians, the GOC Northern Ireland and other British Army officers.

That memories have been recovered without renewed bitterness suggests that some social healing has taken place.

The Healing of Memory
The Irish writer Colm Tóibín is a native of Enniscorthy, Co Wexford. The hill which overlooks Enniscorthy is Vinegar Hill on which the rebels of 1798 made their last stand. The rebellion, beginning with high non-sectarian ideals, turned sectarian and Vinegar Hill, in the weeks when it was held by the rebels, was used as a place where Protestants could be taken to be tortured and killed. The rebellion itself was ruthlessly put down by the British Government.

Tóibin tells the following story:
In 1994, Enniscorthy Cathedral was in need of serious restoration and collections were made to fund the work. It was decided after Easter that the cathedral would close and Mass

would now be said in the local convent and in the large hall owned by the Gaelic Athletic Association. The local Church of Ireland, however, offered the use of their church as well, the one my uncle took over during the Civil War. Most of the people in the town had never been inside this church.

On Saturday, 16 April, then, evening Mass was said to a packed congregation in the Protestant church in Enniscorthy. On the way into the church groups of people were photographed to mark what the priest called 'this historic occasion'. The Protestant church was much smaller than ours, less imposing, and squarer in shape. There was a beautiful marble pulpit with an eagle's head on the lectern. Some stained glass showed Jesus in a red tunic holding a lamb, but the other long windows were made of light green glass.

It was strange to be in a Protestant church seeing familiar Catholic faces and hearing familiar Catholic prayers. All of us looked around until Mass began. It was announced that there would be no sermon. I could not take my eyes off a plaque on the wall to my left. It was to the memory of Archibald Hamilton Jacob, Late Captain of the Loyal Vinegar Hill Rangers, who Departed This Life, December 1836, Aged 66 Years. 'As a Magistrate, He Was Impartial, As a Subject Loyal, As a Soldier Generous and Brave.'

He must have been up there on Vinegar Hill during the battle of 1798, and he must have been around for the slaughter afterwards, which I heard so much about when I was a child. We were in his church now; we had been invited. Protestant service and Mass would be said here this morning. No one else in the congregation seemed very interested in this plaque, or the sectarian legacy. The plaque was a memorial to a past we would not repeat. History, I believed, had come to an end in Enniscorthy.[23]

Because the past can so possess us, it is important that we find ways of letting go what has happened. The following are some of the ways in which this can take place.

GRIEVING

We may need to lament and grieve for what has been lost and done, and acknowledge anger, injustice, bitterness, pain, resent-

ment, disorientation, loss of identity and uncertainty. For this
we need a language; feelings need to be released into words. The
resources available in the biblical language of lament – which
found expression in the corporate grieving connected with the
destruction of Jerusalem and exile in Babylon – and the ritual actions of the faith community could be of help in this. Denise
Ackermann, Professor of Practical Theology at the University of
Western Cape, says:

> Lamenting offers … a language in which to communicate
> pain, grief and to seek God's compassionate presence in the
> work of healing. It is language which should be spoken pub-
> licly and how better can we do this than by retrieving lament
> in the ritual action of the communities of faith.[24]

There can be too much easy and premature talk about reconciliation in the church. Anger, the shout of despair, the wailing of
grief, the pain of devastating loss, the cries for justice and revenge (all heard in the Bible), need to be acknowledged. They
are human realities that cannot be ignored. Repress them and
they will come back in other ways.

At the same time, people can get lost in grief, pain and a sense
of victimhood. Victimhood can even become an identity, and a
moral high ground to occupy for all eternity. But victimhood is
not the end of the story. An important biblical theme is that of
moving through grief to newness. There is no conflict, especially
deadly conflict, that does not involve pain, emptiness and loss.
But endings can also be beginnings and we may be able to move
through grief to newness. In that movement we may find ourselves reviewing the story we tell about ourselves and imagin-
ing ourselves and our world differently. However, in a conflict,
our story is not the only story …

TELLING OUR STORIES

Stories make sense of a community's experience. They use and
express values, beliefs and commitments. They give reasons for
action and they build community and self-identity. In divided
societies stories often conflict; the same events are understood
from a radically different perspective. We need to tell our stories
to each other and listen intently to what we are told – which involves reaching beyond the words – feeling the pain of the other

as transmitted through the 'memory' of their community. This is 'felt' history. Thus, we begin to see from the perspective of the 'other'. We practice what the Croatian theologian Miroslav Volf describes as 'double vision', seeing both 'from here' and 'from there'.[25] It may be that until some of this visiting of the past together is done, people will not be capable of co-operative activity.

The German theologian Geiko Mueller-Fahrenholz describes an exchange of stories between the former German Chancellor Helmut Schmidt and the Soviet leader Leonid Brezhnev, during Brezhnev's visit to Bonn in March 1973:

> On one evening there was a meeting in the residence of Willy Brandt, who was then Chancellor. The atmosphere was cordial until Brezhnev began to recall in great detail some of the atrocities committed by Nazi troops in Russia. Everyone was listening with a mixture of respect and dread, because it was obvious that the Soviet leader had to free himself of these oppressive memories. His words had to be understood as an indication of what it had cost the Russians to come to the capital of Germany – the heart of what had been their most bitter enemy.
>
> Brezhnev spoke for some twenty minutes. Then Schmidt, who was minister of defence at the time, responded by telling his own story, for he had been one of the German soldiers stationed in Russia. He spoke of the schizophrenic situation of German soldiers who did not adhere to the Nazi ideology but had been educated to be patriots and thus felt bound to defend their country. In recalling this encounter nearly 15 years later, Schmidt comes to a revealing conclusion; he writes that this 'exchange of bitter memories greatly contributed to the mutual respect' that existed between him and Brezhnev, despite the fact that the two found themselves in opposite camps from that evening up to the end of their terms of office.[26]

Working through history together implies rewriting history textbooks together, e.g. the German-Polish Textbook Commission. It may lead us to look at our symbols – anthems, rituals, songs, festivals, special occasions – and the stories and memories in these symbols. It may challenge us to recount the founding events of our histories in a different way – a way which involves

honouring our dead without the necessity of vengeance or further sacrifice. To recount the founding events of a history in a
different way is to change the nature of a community, perhaps to
expand its compass.

Honest discourse about the past – particularly in the presence of the 'other' – may provide resources for a more hopeful
future. The danger is that we refuse to do this and instead we
search for people and institutions to blame for what has happened. We make ourselves 'whited sepulchres' (Mt 23:27, Authorised Version) hiding our guilt, responsibility and hypocrisy in
proclaiming that we are radically different from the people we
blame.

DEALING WITH THE WOUNDS

People and communities must be given a way of dealing with
their suffering, wounds and grief. There is a need for opportuni-
ties for the past to be addressed symbolically, ritually and litur-
gically, and for social space to be

> provided for people to express to and with each other the
> pain and injustices experienced. Acknowledgement and
> mutual recognition of the legitimacy of their experience is
> decisive in the reconciliation dynamic .[27]

If hurt, pain, anger, guilt, and loss are not dealt with effectively
they will be driven underground, sure to surface in unexpected
and harmful ways.

Forgiveness and acknowledgement of wrongs (including
apology) are interrelated ways of dealing with what has happened, which may be deeply transformative and necessary at
key points in a reconciliation process.

FORGIVENESS IN SITUATIONS OF CONFLICT

The following is the story of Michael McGoldrick whose son
was killed by loyalist paramilitaries:

> We turned on our TV and heard that a taxi driver had been
> murdered. I didn't think it could be anyone who belonged to
> us or we would have heard. But the news report continued,
> 'Taxi driver, married with one child, wife expecting another
> baby ...' My wife, Bridie, and I just looked at each other in
> cold denial. Then the next sentence came, 'He just graduated
> from university on Friday.' It was our son.

We rushed out through the door of our house, I hit the ground on my knees and in desperation started pounding my fists. I looked up and cried, 'Hanging on a cross is nothing compared to what we are going through!' Then I looked to my wife and said, 'We'll never smile again.'

The next day, Bridie and I made the decision to take our own lives, because Michael was everything we had. Bridie suffers from arthritis, and had plenty of tablets. But as I went out to the kitchen, suddenly a picture of the crucified Christ came into my mind. It hit me that God's Son too had been murdered – for us. I knew that what we planned to do was wrong. It still amazes me how God intervened in such a miraculous way to change our minds.

Before they closed my son's coffin, I laid my hands on his and said, 'Goodbye, son, I'll see you in heaven.' At that very moment I experienced the power of God coursing through my body. I was filled with a great sense of joy and confidence in God. I felt as if I could have faced Goliath – I never felt as strong in my whole life.

On the morning of the funeral, I wrote on the back of an envelope a word which came to me so calm and clear, referring to those who had murdered Michael: 'Bury your pride with my son.' At the bottom I wrote: 'Forgive them.' I felt that, despite the agony we were going through, God had given me a message of peace, forgiveness and reconciliation. I spoke that message in front of the TV cameras that morning, and I still stand by it. Every morning I ask God to continue to give me the grace to forgive those who murdered my child.[28]

The following is the story of Una O'Higgins O'Malley whose father Kevin O'Higgins, the Irish Free State's Minister for Justice and External Affairs, was murdered in 1927 and her grandfather before that:

No one ever spoke to her about forgiveness, she says; it was 'imprinted' in her. The men who shot her grandfather in his home, for being the father of Kevin O'Higgins, were almost certainly neighbours and known to her grandmother. Yet she would never identify them and insisted on forgiveness and no reprisals. Four years later, when Una was five months old, her father was shot on his way to Sunday Mass. During his five conscious hours, he too chose not to identify his killers, speaking only about forgiveness.

Sixty years later, it would be revealed that Kevin – with eight bullets in him – had managed to speak to his assailants on the roadside, telling them that he forgave them, that he understood why they had done it, but that this must be the end of the killings. There was some doubt that this occurred, but later, one of the attackers, Bill Gannon – who told this to his son – would only speak of O'Higgins as a 'very misunderstood man' and would no longer carry a gun.

But what of another of the gang, Archie Doyle, who had danced on her father's grave? 'I discovered about that while leafing through Uinseann McEoin's book in an airport bookshop in 1987 and I got seized with this awful, awful unforgiving cloud, that I hadn't ever felt as badly before. I couldn't stop it, it was like this lava pouring from a volcano … I had so often gone to that grave. That happened on Holy Thursday and I thought "so much for Holy Thursday and Jesus Christ and all that". I wanted to throw the whole thing out there and then. But on Good Friday, I made my way back to the church somehow and, as I put my foot on the church porch, I had this thought – "Have a Mass said for them all." And that was when I felt normal again …' And so it happened that 60 years after the murder of Kevin O'Higgins, his daughter arranged a memorial Mass in Booterstown church for him and his killers, including Archie Doyle.[29]

These are wonderful stories. At the same time we have to understand the sense of outrage of many victims and survivors at those they see as responsible. An extreme example is the Mothers of the Plaza de Mayo in Argentina who have refused any form of reparation or compensation. They will not participate in any official investigations. They insist that 'you took them away alive, we want them back alive'. Brandon Hamber says:

Perhaps part of their refusal may involve wanting others to experience the frustration they have felt. They are determined to offer constant reminders that, in reality, there is nothing that can ever be done to replace their 'missing' loved ones.[30]

Those who have been directly affected by wrong or by violence may be able to forgive. However, people cannot be burdened with the demand that they forgive. Nor can anyone forgive on behalf of those who have suffered. We cannot impose forgiveness on people, but conditions can be created whereby forgiveness becomes at least a possibility. Public acknowledgement of wrongs inflicted may be of importance in encouraging forgiveness. However, we may have to recognise that there are situations of such suffering that talk of forgiveness may simply be inappropriate and that what is required is solidarity and compassion, perhaps expressed in silence – and in gesture.

Victims have their particular needs: for justice, for the seriousness of the harm to be acknowledged, for apology and repentance from those who have done them wrong, for their stories to be heard, for compensation, for practical support. They have a claim upon our respect, to be remembered and allowed to remember. The past cannot be put right, but we can seek to ensure that it is not repeated. This is one form of memorial to the victims of violence. The challenge for the society is not only to deal with the hurt in the most constructive way possible, but also to learn to cope with and accept as legitimate the ongoing anger and even impossible demands of victims, victims of all sorts of different hues who may have clashing and competing views about who are the 'real' perpetrators and 'real' victims in the situation. This is particularly evident in a divided society.

What is also required is that the larger community – battered, hurt and damaged by what has happened – be prepared to enter into a more general process of being able to set aside the past – with all its enmities, resentments and demands for revenge and sense of victimhood – and start anew, accepting and respecting the existence of the other. This is something in the nature of forgiveness. As the former Zambian President, Kenneth Kaunda, said, forgiveness is not so much an isolated act but 'a constant willingness to live in a new day without looking back and ransacking the memory for occasions of bitterness and resentment'.[31]

Such a process of communal forgiveness takes what happened seriously; thus, truth seeking and telling are important. It does not trivialise or condone violence and injustice. Guilt and responsibility remain. What such a process does do is seek to bring peace to the past for the sake of the present and the future. The goal is healing and a move forward into new relationships. It is about rebuilding what has been torn to pieces, establishing justice, creating trustworthy and sustainable structures and providing secure social spaces for people. Such forgiveness is made easier when there is evidence of people acting in new ways, e.g. decisively moving away from violence or being prepared to negotiate new and just political arrangements, or when regret or apology is expressed for what has happened.

Donald Shriver has presented a powerful case that the American Black Civil Rights Movement is an example of forgiveness 'present in the dynamic of a political process'.[32] Shriver has argued that a process of political forgiveness is marked by forbearance from revenge, empathy for opponents, concern for moral truth and a desire for positive co-existence. He illustrates all of this – most notably the determination to keep the Movement non-violent under the leadership of Martin Luther King and 'the willingness to count oneself as a neighbour and fellow citizen with enemies, in spite of the latter's continuing resistance to reciprocating.'[33]

Some white Americans came to repent:

The story of how some white Americans in this era came to repent of their racist attitudes may never be fully told, but such repentance was the other side of the willingness of many blacks to forgive the past on condition that whites would collaborate in the building of a new political future for Americans of all ethnic origins. Whether on a bus or in a once segregated park or behind closed doors, some whites in Birmingham learned in this period to see their black neighbours with unprecedented empathy. They began to stumble into new relationships on many levels including the political.[34]

And the old South cracked open – and people changed, willingly or unwillingly, even if it was only their actions, and not their thoughts. Vincent Harding, a journalist who covered the Movement, says:

Now, largely as a result of the movement King represented, as a result of the significant developments since his death, the old America has been cracked, wedged open, cannot be the same again. Now, the forces which were absent from the first official beginning of America, in the days following 4 July 1776 – the blacks, the women, the Native Americans, the Chicanos, the students and many more – all who were then pressed aside are now present, are all more aware of themselves, of ourselves, than ever before. King helped create the possibility that all of us might break beyond our own individual and group interests and catch a vision of a new America, create a vision of a new common good in a new future which will serve us all. He saw that our needs were economic and spiritual, political (and moral, social and personal), and as the end approached, he was groping his way towards a new integration …'[35]

Of course, this new society is yet to be fully achieved. The Senator Lott affair of December 2002, when the Senator suggested at the 100th birthday of Senator Strom Thurmond that the US would have been better off if the arch-segregationist had won the Presidency in 1948, shows the continuing ambiguities and uncertainties and the continuing power of the novelist William Faulkner's warning: 'The past is never dead. It's not even past.' But Senator Lott had to resign as Republican Leader in the Senate.

If we fail to forgive, we will hand on our bitterness to the next generation. And, if the politics of grievance is not given up, the past keeps everyone in its grip. Either we find ways to forgive or else we separate from, or seek to destroy, each other. Thus, forgiveness is a practical necessity for continuing to live together. As Rabbi Jonathan Sachs says, 'I forgive because I have a duty to the future no less than the past – to my children as well as my ancestors.'[36]

REPENTANCE

'One of humanity's most intractable problems is self-deception.'[37]

Whole societies, and in particular their dominant groups, engage in forms of cruelty, discrimination, repression or exclusion which are 'known' about but never openly acknowledged. Collusion, denial, silence, self-justification and indifference operate in a complex pattern of 'knowing' and 'not-knowing'. When challenged people resort to arguments of denial ('there is no problem', 'it never happened'); ignorance ('I never knew');

necessity ('it couldn't be other', 'we had to do it'); blaming the other ('it's their fault); mitigation ('but what about what they did to us'); minimising ('there were only ... killed'); epistemological failure on the challenger's part ('you don't, can't, understand'); rationalisation ('it's got nothing to do with me'); exceptionalism ('it's different here'); evasion ('it's difficult to explain'); and victimhood ('we are the real victims in this situation').

Repentance represents a breaking out of silence, denial, false innocence, and evasion, and the pain and shame of acknowledging guilt, into honest speech (Havel's 'living outside the lie'). It represents a naming and confronting of difficult issues. Repentance takes issues of culpability and accountability seriously.

Repentance means: stopping what we are doing; recognition; examination and acknowledgement of wrong doing; accepting responsibility; expressing remorse; finding another way; seeking forgiveness; and seeking to repair the harm done. Repentance involves turning and changing one's ways. A recognition of an other's suffering may be the first step to repentance.

Clearly we are not responsible for, or guilty of, acts we have not done, or in which we have not been directly involved. At the same time, we belong to groups, communities and nations that have done things which were wrong, in the distant or more immediate past. Our history has often imposed suffering on others and often brought benefits to ourselves. We cannot run away from this history and its consequences, for we are caught up in it, even if we are not personally guilty. There is an inter-generational aspect of suffering which has to be taken into account. The past affects present realities and relationships. Thus, there is a solidarity in sin, which involves the living and the dead.

We have duties in relation to the past. As the philosopher Alasdair MacIntyre says in his book *After Virtue:*

> I inherit from the past of my family, my city, my tribe, my nation a variety of debts, inheritances, rightful expectations and obligations. I am born with a past; and to try to cut myself off from that past is to deform my present relationships. The possession of an historical identity and the possession of a social identity coincide.[38]

Geiko Mueller-Fahrenholz writes about German young people born long after the Second World War:

They had no direct involvement in it, yet the sufferings of their parents and grandparents constitute their heritage. They are part and parcel of that bitter bondage because they are victims of their parents' victimisation. Consequently, they need to be set free too. They also wait for acts of total disclosure to break the chains of mistrust, cynicism and revenge that lock generations together. They too are waiting for the demons of the past to be cast out.[39]

Of course there is a complexity about issues in relation to group injustices. There is the issue of whether and to what extent present institutions and governmental actors are responsible for the past.[40] The complexity is not only in relation to the past. Group injustices in the present require the co-operation and co-ordination of many people. They require ideologists; they require organisers and foot-soldiers. They require people to acquiesce, stand idly by and be indifferent, and so on. I discuss some of this later. However, the fact of this complexity does not mean that the representative acknowledgement of wrongs done by politicians and other community leaders is unimportant. On the contrary, it can have a powerful effect, both on the group they lead and on the opposing group.

Acknowledgement of wrongs done and hurts caused represents a facing of the reality of what a particular group, community or nation has done and an acceptance of responsibility. Acknowledgement of what has happened, a willingness to review the story we tell about ourselves, a sense of regret and a disapproval of past actions by our group or community, open up the possibility of new relationships in the present.

Donald Shriver, author of *An Ethic for Enemies*, says that post-1945 German history convinces him that there is such a thing as repentance in a nation's life and that political leaders play a major role in cultivating such repentance. In a memorable 1985 speech, German President Richard von Weizsäcker gave a 'lengthy, unflinching, excuseless enumeration of Nazi crimes and many degrees of association with those crimes by millions of Germans in the years 1933-1945.' 'It was widely believed to be the first time a senior West German leader had publicly challenged the widely heard justification that ordinary Germans

were unaware of the Holocaust'[41] and much else about the aims
of the Nazi regime.

Geiko Mueller-Fahrenholz tells of a letter he received in
November 1993 from Ratu Meli Vesikkulu, an indigenous chief
in Fiji, who supported the military coups there (already referred
to in Chapter Five). The letter tells a story of repentance and forgiveness:

> In the racial violence in my country following the two mili-
> tary coups of 1987, I stood up strongly for the cause of my
> people using violent means to gain the upper hand against
> Indian people who made up the second major race in Fiji.
>
> In 1988, I found a change of heart through the help of a
> church minister first of all, and later through coming in con-
> tact with men and women from Moral Rearmament. Through
> change, I found new humility and obedience, which eventu-
> ally led me to apologise publicly to Indian leaders and lead-
> ers of other races in Fiji for my part in the violence, and to my
> own people for leading them in the wrong direction. Their
> forgiveness of me gave birth to a new spirit, literally, which
> was so powerful in bringing about healing and reconciliation
> among different peoples of Fiji. As the spirit grew, trust was
> rebuilt and barriers taken down, leaders began to talk and
> govern fairly, and stability and security returned.
>
> This incident was a big factor in Fiji going beyond vio-
> lence to a caring and sharing society, and the restoration of
> democracy through our first general election last year ...
>
> There is much more to be done ... to ensure that this spirit
> of forgiveness lives and thrives in the hearts of our people for
> always. Of course we have problems, but the spirit of restitu-
> tion and forgiveness is helping to rebuild and reinforce the
> moral fibre of our nation, which will ensure a brighter future
> for our children ...[42]

Former Bosnian Serb President Biljana Plavsic pleaded guilty in
October 2002 at the International Criminal Court for the former
Yugoslavia at The Hague. A former biology professor she was
nicknamed the 'Iron Lady' during the war years and became
famous for justifying the murder of Muslims on the grounds
that they were biologically inferior to Serbs. In a document setting out facts underpinning her guilty plea, Plavsic acknowl-

edged she covered up crimes, ignored allegations of criminal acts and 'publicly rationalised and justified the ethnic cleansing of non-Serbs'.[43] She accepted what a statement calls her 'responsibility and remorse fully and unconditionally'. She said her acknowledgement of guilt is 'individual and personal' but appealed to 'others, especially leaders, on any side of the conflict to examine themselves and their conduct'. Plavsic's admission of guilt is 'the first crack in what has been a stonewall denial of what happened in Bosnia, and of any responsibility by defendants in The Hague and across Serbian society in general.' There are indications that Plavsic's deep Christian faith may have played a major role in her decision to plead guilty.

There may also be implicit repentance. Solomon Schimmel suggests that to be

> willing to make peace with an enemy when under no duress to do so suggests a measure of empathy for him and perhaps a willingness to concede that there is some justification for his animosity if not for his behaviour. It may also suggest a willingness to be sufficiently self-critical of one's own position, to concede that what one's own group has done hasn't always been justifiable. These are early stages of repentance.[44]

Schimmel also writes about the effects of Sadat's visit to Israel and how there were elements of repentance in it:

> ... I was in Israel in 1977 and personally recall experiencing the profound and dramatic effect that Anwar Sadat's 1977 visit to Jerusalem and the Israeli Knesset (Parliament) had on many Israeli Jews. They had longed for acknowledgement on the part of Arab nations of their suffering and persecution by the Germans and others, and for recognition of their right to a sovereign Jewish state in part of the historic homeland of the Jews. Sadat's actions, and the dignified way in which he related to and spoke of Israel and its citizens, pierced layers of fear and resentment toward Egypt and paved the way for Israeli willingness to withdraw from the Sinai Peninsula as part of its peace treaty with Egypt. After a visit to Yad Vashem, the Israeli museum that memorialises the six million Jewish victims of the Holocaust, Sadat said, with regard to Hitler's war against the Jews:

'I had always thought it was exaggerated for mere propa-
ganda. But seeing the portrayals and exhibits strength-
ened my determination to achieve peace for those who
suffered the tragedy. I saw with my own eyes how
Israelis, and Jews the world over, must feel. They are victims not of war alone but also of politics and hatred.'

Sadat did not apologise or repent, nor did Israelis forgive
him and Egypt, for the wars that these two nations fought.
Yet elements of repentance were implicit in these interactions, or were perceived as such by many Israelis. Sadat's
visit of a few days softened decades of accrued animosity.[45]

APOLOGY

Acknowledgement of wrongs done and hurts caused may take
the form of apology. Apology is the verbalised face of repentance. It opens up the possibility of reconnection with the 'other'.
The following are some examples of apologies by political leaders:

• 'As President of Russia, and on behalf of the Russian people and the Government, I would like to express my apology for
these inhuman acts' (Russian President, Boris Yeltsin, on internment of Japanese POWs after the Second World War, October
12, 1993).

• 'I took this opportunity to express my deep remorse as well
as to apologise for the fact that Japan's past actions had inflicted
deep wounds on many people, including the former prisoners of
war' (Japanese Prime Minister, Morihiro Hosekawa, after meeting with John Major, September 20, 1993).

• 'If I could do anything about it, I would have liked to have
avoided it. Yes, we say we are sorry' (President F. W. de Klerk
on apartheid, April 29, 1993).

• 'We took the traditional lands and smashed the traditional
way of life. We committed the murders. It was our ignorance
and prejudice and failure to imagine these things done to us'
(Australian Prime Minister, Paul Keating speaking about the
Aborigines, December 1992).

• The State failed in its obligations 'whether by tolerating social discrimination, failing to heed the message of the persecuted,
failing to offer refuge to those who sought it, or failing to con-

front those who openly or covertly offered justification for the prejudice and race hatred which led to the Shoah. And I think it appropriate today, holding the office that I do, to formally ac-knowledge the wrongs that were covertly done, by act and omission, by some who exercised the executive power in our society in breach of the spirit of the Constitution' (The Irish Republic's Minister for Justice, Michael McDowell, January 2003).

After the Second World War, 2.7 million ethnic Germans were expelled from Czechoslovakia. Their property was seized. Many were murdered. All were turned into refugees. This followed Munich and the German dismemberment of Czechoslovakia in 1938 and subsequent invasion in 1939. In 1996 the German Government apologised for Nazi 'policies of violence' and the Czech Government, in turn, expressed regret that the expulsion of the Sudeten Germans had 'caused suffering and injustice to innocent people'.

Apology – clearly and publicly expressed – is one way of say-ing to people that we wish to make a break with the past. Of course, apology has to be followed by, or linked to, an attempt to undo wrongs and act differently – to establish a new justice and a new relationship. And it involves risk and vulnerability.

Public rituals of atonement are important to help individuals come to terms with the painfulness of their society's past, for their healing and for reconciliation. As Michael Ignatieff says about one example of such symbolic politics:

> When President Alwyn of Chile appeared on television to apologise to the victims of Pinochet's crimes of repression, he created the public climate in which a thousand acts of private repentance and apology became possible. He also symbolic-ally cleansed the Chilean State of its association with these crimes.[46]

For apology to have power it must be made by leaders who have credibility and a capacity to be considered representative, both by the group they are apologising on behalf of, and by the com-munity to whom they are apologising. Timing is important; there are particular moments when words of apology speak. Too soon and often the apology is not believed: the pain, hurt

and anger of the victims appear not to have been taken seriously
– some work of mourning needs to have taken place. The
groundwork needs to have been done and this is where non-
governmental activity can be important. Place and context are
important, as is an audience willing to respect and hear the
speaker. Apology also needs to be set in the context of a process
of establishing a new relationship. And the words chosen are
important, because apology publicly puts on record the fact of
violation and accepts or fixes responsibility. It also implicitly or
explicitly promises that similar acts will not be repeated in future.
An apology can be 'a prelude to reconciliation'. Forgiveness is
implied in the positive responses that follow apologies or in the
actions of an offended country or group that precede it.
However, an apology may not be accepted, or those who have
been wronged may not be around to forgive. All of this does not
make an apology valueless, nor does it make better relationships
impossible.

Apologies are speech acts and we have to be attentive to their
contents. The British Prime Minister Tony Blair apologised for
British irresponsibility in the 1840s over the Irish Famine.
Cardinal Cahal Daly has asked forgiveness from the British people on behalf of the Irish people for injuries suffered at the hands
of Irish terrorists. Tony Blair was not responsible for failing to
act to alleviate the Irish Famine, nor was Cardinal Daly responsible for the IRA campaign of violence. Neither person was apologising for something that they had in fact done.

The theologian Nigel Biggar argues that Tony Blair was in effect saying:

Although there is continuity at various levels between the
British State today and the British State then, there is discon-
tinuity in the moral evaluation of Britain's handling of the
Irish famine (and, given the famine's status as a token, of
Ireland as a whole). We British today recognise that we failed
to do what we should have done. We therefore publicly accept your judgement upon us, and distance ourselves now
from ourselves then. Thereby we hope to assure you that our
negligence in the past does not betoken our negligence in the
present or in the future.[47]

Likewise, Cardinal Daly was saying something like this:

> We, the vast majority of Irish people, publicly repudiate
> what some have perpetrated in our name. We do not want
> you to confuse us with them, nor the current and future rela-
> tions between our peoples to be distorted by such confusion.
> Know that we agree with you in your moral evaluation of
> republican violence, and that therefore you can trust us.[48]

Symbolic actions may be more important than any words; for instance the West German Chancellor Willy Brandt falling to his
knees at a monument to those who died in the Warsaw ghetto
rising. Brandt witnessed to a world beyond power and politics,
and to the need for atonement. He vicariously identified himself
completely with the history of the nation (an astonishing action
because he had been a resistance fighter against Hitler).

Demands for apology are often part of a claim for justice and
respect. An acknowledgement that a wrong has been done is important. But demands for apology are often counter-productive
and can feed resentment. They are frequently seen as an attempt
to humiliate the other party. Apology cannot come about and do
its work where people are defensive or where legalism takes
precedence over moral imperatives, or where apology is part of
some power game. Apologies best arise out of a process of free,
honest and authentic reflection, and not from moral blackmail.
Apologies – even murmurs of regret – should be received in a
forgiving spirit with a lack of self-righteousness. After all, there
is 'none righteous no, not one' (Rom 3:10, Authorised Version).
Everyone is a sinner (which does not mean that all have sinned
equally), all groups have committed wrongs in their history. The
aim should be new relationships, not moral (or other) victories.
A process of reconciliation cannot take place if it is approached
from a position of self-righteousness, apportioning blame and
claiming innocence.

TRUTH

It has been argued that it is important for a public account to be
rendered of what happened and who was responsible. Wrongdoing and injustice are publicly acknowledged. Building a trustworthy peace, it has been contended, requires honest discourse
about the past. Thus, Truth Commissions have been established
in such countries as South Africa, Chile, El Salvador and
Guatamala.

Of central importance is that these Truth Commissions were official attempts at truth-telling and truth-learning. They arise from, or are part of, a peace process and often incorporated political compromises. Thus, in South Africa, amnesty was given to perpetrators in return for public disclosure. The perpetrators were held to account but they were not punished if they disclosed what they had done. Signs of contrition or apologies were not required, even though they did take place on some occasions. The victims were able to publicly tell their story, and for some of the families of victims there was the possibility of finding out what happened to their loved ones. Through these processes the victims and their families were given respect and the possibility of the restoration of personal and civil dignity. A process such as this may be sufficient for many people to put the past behind them. What was given up, however, was the possibility of punitive justice against the perpetrators. This was not uncontroversial. Some victims or their families were totally opposed to the granting of amnesty and challenged this in court.

Rwanda has also instituted a public confessional process but one in which punitive justice is not given up. Prisoners classified as 'Category One' killers – some 2,500 genocide planners, well-known murderers, or those who killed with 'zeal' or 'excessive wickedness' – will be tried eventually in Rwanda's regular courts. If convicted, even their heartfelt confessions will not spare them the maximum sentence of life imprisonment or death. But during the next five years, the great majority of prisoners will appear before a *gacaca* jury of their peers, people elected by the community as 'persons of integrity'. The community judges will rely on evidence provided by the people living in Rwanda at the time of the genocide who are mandated by law to turn up at the once-a-week hearings. Those who confess murder – even serial murder – and who are deemed to have faithfully and remorsefully recounted the details of their participation, could see their sentences halved from fourteen years' to just seven years' jail time and seven years' community service. For most who have been locked up since the genocide, this will mean immediate release. If an inmate does not confess, and the *gacaca* judges find him guilty, he will be sentenced to anywhere from twenty-five years to life. The later a prisoner's confession comes in the *gacaca* process, the less of a sentence reduction he or she will receive. A central aim of the *gacaca* process is to stimulate a social conversation and establish what actually happened during the killing frenzy of 1994.

It is worth noting that the whole idea that nations should systemically and publicly face up to their difficult past has only been commonplace since 1945. Before that, forgetting was encouraged. European peace treaties, from one between Ludwig of Germany, Charles of France and Lothar of Lotharingia in 853 to the Treaty of Lausanne in 1923, solemnly required an act of forgetting between former enemies. The argument has been that 'mankind cannot bear too much reality' and that merciful oblivion is the best approach. We decreasingly take this approach and seek truth.

However, truth itself has many layers. The South African Truth and Reconciliation Commission worked with four notions of truth: factual or forensic; personal and narrative; social or 'dialogue'; healing and restorative.

- *Factual or forensic truth:* legal or scientific information which is factual, accurate and objective and is obtained by impartial procedures. At the individual level this means information about particular events and specific people: what exactly happened to whom, where, when and how. At the societal level, it means recording the context, causes and patterns of violations: an interpretation of facts that should at least erode any denials about the past. Disinformation once accepted as truth must lose its credibility.
- *Personal and narrative truth:* the stories told by perpetrators and (more extensively) victims. This is an opportunity for the healing potential of testimony, for adding to the collective truth and for building reconciliation by validating the subjective experience of people who had previously been silenced or voiceless.
- *Social truth:* the truth generated by interaction, discussion and debate. The hearings provide transparency and encourage participation. Conflicting views about the past can be considered and compared. It is the process that matters, rather than the end result.
- *Healing and restorative truth:* the narratives that face the past

in order to go forward. Truth as a factual record is not enough: interpretation must be directed towards goals of self-healing, reconciliation and reparation. This requires the acknowledgement that everyone's suffering was real and worthy of attention.[49]

In these four notions of truth, both truth-telling and truth-learning are involved. In truth-learning the truth of what has been done is confronted, in particular *we* confront what *we* have done. But there is a further, deeper dimension to truth-learning: we confront the reality of (our) wrong-doing. Thus the issue of moral judgement has to be faced. For participants in a bitter and protracted conflict, issues of truth-learning and the associated moral judgement are extremely difficult to face. Denial is the easier option.

Truth needs to be publicly established. This is why the creation of Truth Commissions in some situations has been significant. Judicial inquiries and court cases have been important in particular circumstances. However the difficulties, particularly in contested spaces, need to be understood.

It may be that a public account of what has happened and who was responsible can be rendered. However, rendering a public account of what has happened and who was responsible does not free us from conflicting interpretations, clashing memories, etc, about the past, or even disagreement about what the conflict has been about. Focusing on specific events may bring its own distortions and community anger (why this event? why not this one? etc). 'Truths' about the past may continue to be disputed. Nor does truth-telling necessarily lead to healing and reconciliation (certainly not at once). Indeed, truth can be used as a weapon directed against political opponents and as a means to claim superiority in a political struggle. It can open up old wounds and reinforce division. What may be hoped for by rendering a public account is that the range of permissible 'truths' may be narrowed and that particular lies, silences, fictions, myths and denials are effectively challenged. After the South African Truth and Reconciliation Commission no one could honestly deny that apartheid was a monstrous crime.

What all of this points to is a longer term need for work to be done on the reconciling of stories and memories, so that there is a recognition of the inter-dependence of our histories and of what we have done to each other. New realities, critical and moral reflection, spiritual transformation, changed relationships and time may open up the possibility of some shared truth being established.

Is a Truth Commission Mechanism Suitable for Northern Ireland?
Truth Commissions are grounded in a peace process and appear to work best when there is a powerful political consensus that 'truth' must be established. The context of a fragile peace like Northern Ireland's, where the conflict continues to smoulder on, may be unpropitious. Nevertheless, the issue is not whether a Truth Commission is needed but how to deal with the past, and how to finish with what has happened.

The Report of the Healing Through Remembering Project[50] proposes that a formal truth recovery process should be given careful consideration. It suggests that an important first step in a process of truth recovery would be acknowledgement by all organisations and institutions that have been engaged in the conflict of their responsibility for past political violence.

There have been fragments of acknowledgement so far – limited apologies by the loyalist paramilitaries and the IRA, David Trimble's statement that 'it was a cold house for Catholics' in his Nobel Prizewinner's speech. The Stevens Report (April 2003) lifted a veil on collusion between the security forces and loyalist paramilitaries in the murder of innocent Catholics. The revelation about a top British Army agent in the Provisional IRA (May 2003) shone further light on the 'dirty war' on terrorism: the value of the intelligence provided apparently required the State's agents to collude in torture and murder.[51] The results of the Saville Inquiry into the events of Bloody Sunday in Derry in 1972 are yet to come. There may be inquiries into other disputed events. However, the Good Friday Agreement carefully side-stepped issues of guilt and responsibility and the demand for truth far exceeds supply. Huge holes are left in some people's biographies and we make do with implicit repentance in the commitment to peaceful politics and the acceptance of political and social change in others. Implicit forgiveness is expressed in a willingness to work with former bitter enemies. Perhaps truth will emerge piecemeal over time rather than in any structured way – 'a patchwork quilt of truth'.

The dilemmas are acute. On the one hand John Kelly, whose brother was killed on Bloody Sunday, says 'The cost for the search for truth and justice should be immaterial.'[52] On the other hand, the Chief Constable, Hugh Orde, said, regarding the re-cently re-activated inquiry into the 1972 IRA bomb which killed nine people in the Co Londonderry village of Claudy, he was 'investigating so much history' at a time when his force was very short of detectives. Orde also pointed out that only thirty percent of murders of police officers during the 'troubles' had been solved. He then went on to say, 'If the government wants me to start looking backwards, then I'll look backwards across the board.' The claims of the past *versus* the claims of the present and the future; and the demands of equity in dealing with differ-ent cases: such are the dilemmas. And all resentments and injustices cannot be addressed.

RESTITUTION

Restitution is the restorative aspect of justice. We can never undo and make good the evil that has been done; in this sense strict restorative justice is impossible. We can seek to repair the damage that has been done, where that is possible. However, restitution should be seen more as an act of compensation that fulfils certain functions in the present: firstly, as a sign of recog-nition of the seriousness of what has happened; secondly, as a sign of the seriousness of repentance; thirdly, it meets some need of the victim; and fourthly, it aims at facilitating a more human future. Recognition and respect are given to the victim, or their memory.

The idea of restitution has become increasingly important in national and international politics, for instance in relation to the Holocaust, the treatment of indigenous peoples in Australia, New Zealand and the United States, and the internment of Japanese Americans during the Second World War. The process of negotiating restitution agreements has involved a process of dialogue – a social conversation – between victims and perpetra-tors about the meaning of events. It brings new recognitions about intertwined pasts, about inclusion, about injustices and the need to right wrongs – if only partially. Such a process opens up the possibility of reconciliation.

PUNISHMENT

Punishment is the punitive aspect of justice. We cannot do without some form of punitive institutionalised response to wrongdoing, no matter how inadequate and imperfect it may be. Punishment of the perpetrator is a statement that the injured person matters, that justice matters. Through the criminal justice system, the perpetrator is called to account and held responsible for their misdeeds. The truth of what happened is hopefully revealed and there is the possibility of the victim's story being told. The perpetrator pays for what he/she has done and this is reflected in the seriousness of the sentence. Retribution takes place. Punishment is one way respect is shown to the victims (and their families). And punishment helps restore the moral order of society.

Punishment necessarily individualises guilt. In the context of community conflict (e.g. former Yugoslavia, Rwanda, Sierra Leone) the pursuit of justice through the legal system is an ambiguous and frustrating activity – for instance, difficulties can arise from selective prosecutions and this can undermine perceptions of fairness. The courtroom focus on specific individuals and specific events can distort. Important issues such as why something happened, the chains of responsibility, and the hidden cultural or social triggers, can be lost within the confines of the courtroom. Trials of particular war criminals can too easily close off the past, with broader issues of responsibility not faced up to.

The issue of responsibility is complex. President Havel of the Czech Republic said of the situation in Eastern Europe:

> The Communist system was uniquely able to suck everybody in. So responsibility for everything was devolved on everyone and nobody could take all the blame, as the case might be in a conventional dictatorship.[53]

A whole society became contaminated. Nevertheless, there is a particularity of responsibility as well.

Community conflict creates a context where there are all sorts of degrees and categories of guilt: that of the ideologues who promote hate and prepare the ground for violence; that of those who plan and direct acts of violence; that of those who plant bombs and pull triggers; that of helpers and supporters; that of people who condone and benefit; that of those who are bystanders; and so on. There are sins of omission and sins of commission. There are the sins of people who journeyed into the far country of violence. There are the sins of the people who stayed 'at home', who remained law abiding but who have been consumed by anger, resentment, self-righteousness and the refusal of generosity. There are the misdeeds of groups, e.g. paramilitaries, and there are the misdeeds of the state, its agencies and agents.

An aspect of all of this is the systemic – the trans-individual – reality of evil, something particularly evident in conflict situations. This reality generates its own momentum and logic. Part of the dynamic is the seductiveness of violence and its endless justifications, and the fear, dread, hatred, excitement and frenzy which carry people along, 'the diabolic forces lurking in all violence'[54] in the words of the German sociologist Max Weber.

This is not to say that we make no distinctions between actors, actions and activities – for this we must do. Clearly some have suffered far more than others. Some individuals, groups and institutions have killed and injured far more than others, and thus carry more guilt and responsibility. Horrendous actions are not automatic, or even 'understandable', responses to someone else's behaviour, or to injustice, or to history, or to the 'system'. Human beings remain moral agents. Conscious options for violence are taken. What I am suggesting is a moral complexity – a tangled web – of which we are all part.

Part of the complexity is the issue of the punishment of perpetrators. On the one hand, the perpetration of violence and injustice – particularly the very worst category of human rights violations – demand punishment, and this is why the granting of amnesty in many countries in South America was greeted with outrage. Impunity means that the past and what happened are not faced up to. There is no accountability and no justice. On the other hand, political necessity and prudence may argue for amnesty, amnesia, forbearance and mercy, so that a new start may be made. Managing a peaceful transition requires deals to be made, the pursuit very often of a very murky path of compromise, the prevalence of ambiguity, and the loose ends of history to be left dangling. For instance, De Gaulle managed the transition in post-war France by pretending that all French citizens had been outstanding patriots; the sorry history of the Vichy regime and collaboration was swept under the carpet. What happens in such situations is that the issue of blame is avoided or displaced elsewhere, and instead the emphasis is put on the present and the future. The consequence is that the difficult moral issues relating to the past are not publicly talked about.

The exigencies of politics and the balance of forces may well push the issue of how the past is to be dealt with in a particular direction. Brandon Hamber says:

> The strategies that are adopted for dealing with the past will inevitably be shaped by the current political context. In South Africa, the balance of forces at the time of transition played a significant role in shaping the 'remembering' process that came afterwards. Given the nature of the negotiated settlement, it was impossible to undertake large-scale prosecutions. Within this context amnesty can be seen as a necessary and unavoidable pre-condition to the negotiated peace settlement. In turn, the 'amnesty' deal shaped and gave rise to the Truth and Reconciliation Commission.[56]

A middle path was chosen between prosecutions and blanket amnesty. Many countries such as Spain, El Salvador, Uruguay, Brazil, and post-Sandinista Nicaragua have opted for blanket or successive amnesties – the path of official forgetting. Others chose selective pardons or laws limiting prosecution, as in Argentina.

The middle path between prosecution and blanket amnesty chosen in South Africa can be seen as a form of collective political forgiveness. The past and its crimes were not officially forgotten. On the contrary, the conditional amnesty process sought to uncover what really happened to the victims and provided a mechanism for the relevant parties to tell their side of the story. This did not mean that particular victims or their families personally forgave, although this process may have helped in some cases.

Similarly the release of politically motivated prisoners on

licence in Northern Ireland can be seen as a form of collective political forgiveness (despite its controversial nature) because it preserved the reality of the offence. Again this does not say anything about whether victims or their families can personally forgive the perpetrators (it may make it harder).

LUSTRATION

The purging of officials of the old regime from public office has been used in some former communist states of Eastern Europe. The problem has been that if such a law is too widely framed then it risks being unfair to particular individuals and raises human rights issues, and if it is too narrowly framed then many culpable people escape. Purges are a symbolic statement of a new start, risk arbitrariness and, therefore, should be confined to the most senior, visible or influential positions in a criminal regime. All those compromised by the past cannot be dealt with punitively; society would simply seize up. The past and issues of responsibility have to be confronted by other means. Societies have to explore the how, when and by whom this is to be done.

OTHER DIMENSIONS OF JUSTICE

Important in the restoration of a moral order is the strengthening of the law and assent to law – legal justice. Thus issues of policing and reform of the legal system are central to social reconstruction. In contested 'spaces' conflict often focuses on the law and order system. In a new dispensation it has to become a common authority above all groups and citizens, rather than supporting the position of one group over and against another.

Issues of distributive justice, dealing with inequalities and promoting human rights, are also of vital importance. Justice is also about having a place, being included in the community, being given what is needed to make a contribution, participating, being taken into account, and being treated as human, i.e. it is about respect. Talk about reconciliation is hollow unless there is real change for those who are socially and economically excluded. Authentic reconciliation involves justice.

But the attempt to solve conflicts by simply establishing justice alone, or by saying first justice then reconciliation, will not work. One of the complexities of enduring conflicts is that the issue of justice gets blurred and deformed in the vicious cycle of action and reaction. The pursuit of justice creates more injustices. Because of disagreements about the past there is no agreement about what constitutes justice and equality in the present. Further, in many conflict situations justice is often not the primary issue. It is the relationship of fear, threat, distrust and even hatred, and what each has done to the other.

It also has to be recognised that groups do not simply lose their histories by the fact of structural change. Resentful histories and mistrustful relationships may simply continue unless people imagine themselves and their relationships afresh. The struggle for justice has to be placed in a context of a wish for recognition of the 'other', social conversation and co-operation, i.e. a perspective of a desire for reconciliation.

A CHRISTIAN ACCOUNT

A Christian account suggests that there has to be a remembering of and a reckoning with the past. It will, however, seek a certain kind of remembering: remembering the past in order that we do not repeat the past's destructiveness, so that we become different people. It will also seek a certain kind of forgetting: forgetting not as amnesia but rather as a release from the full weight and burden of the past. It will also seek a reckoning, but a reckoning that will put an emphasis on creating a new moral order where people belong together in a context where injustice, antagonism and desire for revenge have been taken out of the situation.

In Conclusion

Dealing with the past is likely to be a process rather than an event, and it is likely to take generations. It does not seem likely that simple forgetting is an option. For instance, issues in relation to France's actions in Algeria in the 1950s and 1960s, once thought buried by 'acts of oblivion', are now creeping out into the public domain. At the same time we do not seem able to bear too much truth – because the truth can as easily destroy as liberate. We need a care-taking honesty. And timing is important: 'There is a season for everything ... a time for keeping silent, a time for speaking' (Ecclesiastes 3:7).

CHAPTER SEVEN

Trust and a Reconciled Society

Trust
'Any long-range attempt at constructing a social order ... must be predicated on the development of mutual trust between social actors.'[1]

Political institutions can only operate where there are relationships of trust. They can only function when trust is granted and where politicians and political institutions act in a fashion that generate trust. At the same time, the structuring of society and its institutions deeply influences who you can trust.

Satisfactory government depends upon a complex series of trust relationships between political leaders, political institutions and the population. Politics can only work when politicians use power forbearingly, where they sustain the fabric of the community and allow a place for opponents, and where electorates give room to their politicians to give leadership, recognise the burdens which politicians carry and the forgiveness that they require.

No government or public institution is perfect. Thus political forgiveness from citizens is required to release politicians and institutions from the failure and shortcomings that result from acting in a complex world. But political forgiveness requires that failures and shortcomings are recalled and acknowledged (e.g. through apology). In this way a civic relationship is restored that is worthy of respect, and trust is re-established.

It is the central task of political structures and the law and order system to give security, reliability and predictability to society. Their ritual and routine gives stability and offers the possibility of social trust. Institutions acceptable to the vast majority of citizens are of vital importance because they provide the possibility of social conversation, debate and negotiation of difference taking place in all their messy, conflictual reality.

What is Required to Create Trust?

Some of the factors required are:

- a commitment to exclusively peaceful means ;
- an acknowledgement of the other side's pain and suffering and a recognition of a common humanity;
- a willingness to understand the fears and sense of threat that the other community has and to seek to take them into account, even if they are thought to be groundless;
- a willingness to make conciliatory gestures and actions;
- a willingness to do things that will reduce fear and threat and provide reassurance;
- showing by signs, words and actions a desire for change;
- a willingness to treat the other side with respect and to avoid humiliating them;
- a willingness to meet, to listen, to talk;
- a willingness to be bound by promises and agreements (implicit and explicit) which will be kept;
- a willingness to take the interests and identities of the other community into account;
- identifying mutual self-interests and building on them;
- a willingness to act justly;
- a willingness to provide for the security and well-being of the other community;
- some shared ground or togetherness that will enable conflict and differences to be dealt with;
- a willingness to develop a relationship with other groups, parties and individuals and to co-operate where possible (e.g. on economic and social issues); and
- a willingness to create a stable social order together.

Trust is often tentative and it grows only gradually. Patience and time are required. Trust is usually imperfect: we trust each other enough to argue out our differences but not so much as to forget that our rights and interests may be infringed. That is why groups require protection, safeguards, and external guarantors. Trust is a risk. Completely satisfactory guarantees can never be obtained that the other group and their leaders are trustworthy. Political agreements always involve risk and uncertainty.

Confidence-building is a precursor to the development of trust. It offers the possibility of trust growing. Thus in a conflict situation, finding appropriate confidence-building measures is very important.

Growing trust and mutual recognition enables hard issues to be dealt with, e.g. issues of guilt and responsibility, issues of law and order, and of the decommissioning of weapons.

The issue of trust points to other fundamental issues – those of consent and belonging together. These underlie the workings of democracy and politics.

Consent

A majority's right is relatively – but not totally – uncontroversial in a stable state, i.e. one where the vast majority give their consent to its political arrangements. However, a divided society cannot work without mutual consent or agreement. Thus the winning of consent and the development of cross-community consensus must have a high priority.

Belonging Together

In democracies legitimate government is based on the consent of a whole people who acknowledge their common bond together. Behind this consent, however, lies a deeper and often unstated acknowledgement and acceptance that, despite or in our differences, we belong together, i.e. there is a solidarity in which there is an inter-dependence and a common good. Inter-dependence and a common good require a shared community where we can belong together.

Trust also requires a re-establishment of connections between people, a re-weaving of the social fabric. Political agreements and shared institutions, while vital, are not enough in themselves. Antagonistic divisions need to be overcome. Politicians and other community leaders need to model good relations. Connections between people and social institutions need to be made, connections that involve understanding, respect, familiarity and relationships with the 'other', acceptance, empathy and co-operation. In all of this there is an important role for civil society: churches, business, trade unions, schools, voluntary and community groups. Research shows that there is a correlation between multi-ethnic peace and the existence of cross-community networks of civic associations.[2]

Inter-dependence requires a shared community where we can belong together and co-operate on common activities and in common institutions. In a divided society it is not enough to attend only to issues of equity and diversity – the danger in doing so is that the 'us and them' mind-set is reinforced. Issues of belonging together, of a shared community, of inter-dependence, of mutual recognition, of respect, must also receive consideration. They are vital to social trust and a key to reconciliation.

A Reconciled Society and Issues of Symbolic Expression

Nationhood is about the shared story we tell of ourselves and our forebears. It is also how we are described by a place, sometimes by a language, by historic events, by parades, remembrances, ceremonies, celebrations and monuments, by a flag and an anthem. In a 'normal' state, these are the things that people have in common and that bind them together. In a contested 'space' the same things are often in dispute and pull people apart. What belongs to one community is often hated by the other. These symbolic expressions engage the affective part of ourselves – our emotions – and are profoundly important.

Reconciliation has to be expressed at the symbolic level as well as the institutional level. It will not be enough to create a neutral public or state space. A symbolic deficit will be created which will inhibit a sense of a shared community. Some 'transcendent' symbols and rituals are required to express inter-dependence and a shared community. Symbols and rituals 'work' when they represent something real, so they cannot simply be artificially created. We have to work at 'growing' common symbolic expression as well as developing real relationships of inter-dependence. We also have to recognise that communities require security at the symbolic level as well as at the institutional level.

Concluding Reflections

The language of reconciliation offers a rich language to approach the overcoming of enmity and division, and the healing of wounds. This book has been devoted to exploring the multivocal nature of this language and its many layers, which can encompass the spiritual and moral transformation of individuals and communities, and the political and social transformation of structures that distort human relations. Handling differences, living and belonging together, and trust are part of this language too. Biblical stories have been used to illuminate the meaning of reconciliation. Metaphors like 'embrace' have been explored. The accumulated history of enmity and division leave a terrible memory and I have sought to probe various aspects of remembering.

At the heart of the book has been an exploration of how the complex and multi-stranded weave of forgiveness, justice, truth and repentance can overcome the past. As I have pointed out in the Introduction, reconciliation, forgiveness and repentance are increasingly appearing in political discourse. Philippe Moreau Defarges even suggests that 'repentance has become an essential component of the spirit of the age.'[1] Rodney Petersen, Executive Director of the Boston Theological Institute, says: 'Many in the public policy community in North America now believe that the term forgiveness will be central to working with the political order of the twenty-first century.'[2]

It is certainly true that apologies by political figures have become more numerous and there is more discussion of the significance of forgiveness in political life. We should be careful, however, in overloading this language by claiming too much. Politics remains about power and the advancement of interests. But it is not only about interests and power; politics cannot be divorced from communal and personal attitudes and values. A nation's (and group's) conscious and unconscious memories are the raw material of its policies and politics. How the past is dealt with is of political importance. According to Geiko Mueller-Fahrenholz,[3] 'a nation that is clear and honest about its history can be a trusted covenant partner for its neighbour' (see the discussion about promising and covenant in Chapter One). Presumably the same is true for groups within nations.

Those of us who are Christians can get concerned about the colonisation of 'our' language by the secular world. Hannah Arendt, a secular Jew, has gone so far as to argue that Jesus was 'the discoverer of the role of forgiveness in the realm of human affairs', but then goes on to say that its religious context should not prevent us from taking the discovery seriously in a strictly secular sense. She says that 'Jesus emphasised that the human capacity to forgive should not be reduced to the divine mercy but should be recognised as a genuinely human capacity.'[4] Thus Arendt is arguing that 'our' language of forgiveness is of direct relevance to the secular world. Presumably the same case can be made for reconciliation and repentance.

We may need to be careful that 'our' language is not reduced to purely political language. We will need discernment about the relation of God 'talk' concerning reconciliation to secular 'talk'. We certainly should not assume that there is an unbridgeable chasm between the two discourses – it is better to assume overlap. God works in the world too and linguistic signals – the increasing use of words like reconciliation and forgiveness in the political sphere – may indicate his presence, and that he is telling us something: it is time we Christians were more attentive to the ministry of reconciliation.

Bibliography

For issues in relation to reconciliation:

Eds Gregory Baum and Harold Wells, *The Reconciliation of Peoples: Challenges to the Churches,* World Council of Churches Publications, 1997.

John De Gruchy, *Reconciliation: Restoring Justice,* SCM, 2002.

Eds Alan Falconer and Joseph Liechty, *Reconciling Memories,* The Columba Press, 1998 (2nd edition).

Ed Michael Hurley, *Reconciliation in Religion and Society,* Institute of Irish Studies, 1994.

Michael Ignatieff, *The Warrier's Honor: Ethnic War and the Modern Conscience,* Chatto and Windus, 1998, particularly chapter 'The Nightmare From Which We Are Trying To Awake'.

Joseph Liechty and Cecelia Clegg, *Moving Beyond Sectarianism: Religion, Conflict and Reconciliation in Northern Ireland,* The Columba Press, 2001.

John Paul Lederach, *The Journey Towards Reconciliation,* Herald Press, 1999.

Norman Porter, *The Elusive Quest: Reconciliation in Northern Ireland,* Blackstaff Press, 2003.

Robert Schreiter, *Reconciliation,* Orbis Books, 1996.

Robert Schreiter, *The Ministry of Reconciliation,* Orbis Books, 1998.

Miroslav Volf, *Exclusion and Embrace,* Abingdon Press, 1996.

Articles:

'A Vision of Embrace: Theological Perspectives on Cultural Identity and Conflict', *Ecumenical Review,* April 1995.

'The Social Meaning of Reconciliation', *Interpretation,* 54/2, April, 2000.

For a discussion on restitution:

Elazar Barkan, *The Guilt of Nations: Restitution and Negotiating Historical Injustices*, The Johns Hopkins University Press, 2000.

For the role of Truth Commissions:

Priscilla B Hayner, *Unspeakable Truths: Confronting State Terror and Atrocity*, Routledge, 2001.

For issues in relation to punishment, Truth Commissions, reparations and apology:

Martha Minow, *Between Vengeance and Forgiveness: Facing History after Genocide and Mass Violence*, Beacon, 1998.

For issues in relation to forgiveness:

P. E. Digeser, *Political Forgiveness*, Cornell University Press, 2001.

Evangelical Contribution on Northern Ireland, *Forgiveness Papers* (www. econi.org/ centre).

Eds Raymond Helmick and Rodney Petersen, *Forgiveness and Reconciliation: Religion, Public Policy and Conflict Transformation*, Templeton Foundation Press, 2001.

Richard Holloway, *On Forgiveness*, Canongate, 2002.

Gregory Jones, *Embodying Forgiveness*, Eerdmans, 1995.

Geiko Mueller-Fahrenholz, *The Art of Forgiveness*, World Council of Churches Publications, 1997.

Donald Shriver, *An Ethic for Enemies*, Oxford University Press, 1995.

Donald Shriver, *Forgiveness and Politics: The Case of the American Black Civil Rights Movement*, New World Publications, 1987.

For issues in relation to forgiveness and repentance:

Solomon Schimmel, *Wounds Not Healed by Time: The Power of Repentance and Forgiveness*, Oxford University Press, 2002.

For issues in relation to apology:

Nicholas Tavuchis, *Mea Culpa: A Sociology of Apology*, Stanford University Press, 1991.

For issues in relation to dealing with the past:

Ed Nigel Biggar, *Burying the Past: Making Peace and Doing Justice after Civil Conflict*, Georgetown University Press, 2001.

Erna Paris, *Long Shadows: Truth, Lies and History*, Bloomsbury, 2001.

References and Notes

All Biblical quotations, unless otherwise noted, are from *The Jerusalem Bible.*

INTRODUCTION

1. Porter, *The Elusive Quest: Reconciliation in Northern Ireland,* p 14.
2. Minow, *Between Vengeance and Forgiveness,* p 2.
3. Adapted from Minow, op. cit., p 88.
4. Quoted in *Remembrance and Forgetting: Building a Future in Northern Ireland,* The Faith and Politics Group, 1998.
5. Ibid.
6. Ibid.
7. 'Politics as a Vocation' in Eds H. H. Gerth and A. C. Wright Mills, *From Max Weber: Essays in Sociology,* Oxford University Press, 1958, pp 126-7.
8. Paul Taylor, correspondent for *The Washington Post* in South Africa during the first national election, quoted in *New Pathways: Developing a Peace Process in Northern Ireland,* The Faith and Politics Group, 1997.
9. Shriver, *Forgiveness and Politics,* p 37.
10. P. Petschauer, 'The Diplomacy of Vamik Volkan', *Clios Psychez,* No 1, 1995, pp 34-39.
11. De Gruchy, *Reconciliation,* p 28.

CHAPTER ONE

1. The Irish artist Shane Cullen's sculptural work, *The Agreement,* has digitally routed all 11,500 words of the Agreement into 56 high-density urethane panels, 67 metres long. The meaning of the Agreement is 'shimmery, shifting, contradictory, elusive, multi-faceted' in the words of *The Belfast Telegraph* columnist, Eamonn McCann (May 8, 2003). Texts and art are multi-vocal, like the meaning of reconciliation.
2. Rowan Williams, *On Christian Theology,* Blackwell Publishers, 2000, p 266.
3. For Plavsic quotes see Ed Vulliamy, *The Observer,* December 15, 2002.
4. Parris, *Long Shadows,* p 201.
5. De Gruchy, *Reconciliation,* p 185.
6. Liechty and Clegg, *Moving Beyond Sectarianism,* p 96.

144 THE LAND OF UNLIKENESS

7. Hannah Arendt, *The Human Condition,* University of Chicago Press, 1958, pp 243-7.

8. Joseph Liechty, 'Christian Identity and the Things that Make for Peace', *Lion and Lamb,* January 1996.

9. Ibid.

10. Schreiter, *The Ministry of Reconciliation,* p 118.

11. Volf in 'The Social Meaning of Reconciliation' in *Interpretation,* April, 2000.

12. John Paul Lederach, *Building Peace: Sustainable Reconciliation in a Divided Society,* The United Nations University, 1995, p 52.

13. George Ellis, 'Afterword' in Eds Helmick and Petersen, pp 192-3.

14. Michael Ignatieff, *The Rights Revolution,* House of Anansi Press, 2000, p 141.

15. Michael Ignatieff, *Empire Lite: Nation Building in Bosnia, Kosovo and Afghanistan,* Vintage Original, 2003, p 33.

16. Byron Bland, 'The Post-Troubles Troubles: The Politics of Reconciliation in Northern Ireland', unpublished paper, December 2001.

17. De Gruchy, *Reconciliation,* p 28.

18. Avishai Margalit, *The Ethics of Memory,* Harvard University Press, 2002, p 5.

CHAPTER TWO

1. A speech act creates something that did not exist before the action of speaking it. Examples: A promise is a commitment to do or not to do something or to produce some result. An apology is a declaration of regret which puts on record the fact of violation and accepts and fixes responsibility. It also implicitly or explicitly promises that similar acts will not be repeated in future. One of the aspects of repentance is a declaration of remorse. One of the aspects of forgiveness is a declaration of forgiveness.

2. Chris McGreal, 'Time to Dig up the Hatchet', *The Guardian,* June 10, 1994.

3. Janet Morris, 'Forgiveness and the Individual', *ECONI Forgiveness Papers,* No 11, 2002, p 7.

4. De Gruchy, *Reconciliation,* p 176.

5. Ibid., p 175.

6. See Shriver, *An Ethic for Enemies.*

CHAPTER THREE

1. Marc Gopin, 'The Heart of the Stranger', unpublished paper, Boundaries and Bonds Conference, Stranmillis College, Belfast, June 1997.

2. Miroslav Volf, 'A Vision of Embrace' in *Ecumenical Review,* April, 1995.

3. Ibid.

4. Ibid.

5. Joe Peake, unpublished report, November 1999.

6. What is the relationship between respect and love? Love is mostly used in the context of close inter-personal relationships. Respect is usually used for less close relationships in the social sphere. Hannah Arendt says that respect 'is a regard for the person from the distance which the space of the world puts between us...' and 'what love is in its own, narrowly circumscribed sphere, respect is in the larger domain of human affairs.' Op. cit., p 243.

CHAPTER FOUR

1. In Rembrandt's *Jacob Wrestling with the Angel* it is less a struggle than an embrace. The angel clasps Jacob around the neck and waist with a lover's urgency. At the same time damage is being done. Jacob is having his neck slowly and painfully turned so that he looks the angel in the face.

2. René Girard, *I See Satan Fall Like Lightening*, Orbis Books, 2001, p 111. My interpretation of this story has been heavily influenced by Girard's. See also Keith Clements, *The Churches in Europe as Witnesses to Healing*, WCC Publications, 2003, pp 51-52.

3. See Thomas W. Ogletree, *Hospitality to the Stranger*, Fortress Press, 1985.

4. See in particular, *Violence and the Sacred*, The Johns Hopkins University Press, 1977.

5. Henri Nouwen, *The Return of the Prodigal Son: A Meditation on Fathers, Brothers and Sons*, Doubleday, 1992. When Karl Barth reworked the Christian understanding of salvation in volume IV of his *Church Dogmatics*, one of the fundamental images through which he re-imagined it was the parable of the Prodigal Son, Jesus being daringly identified with the son who wastes his substance in riotous living in a far away country and then returns to the overwhelmingly generous welcome of the father.

6. See Richard Holloway, *On Forgiveness*, pp 79-83.

7. Henri Fischer, 'The Legacy of the Reconciliation Groups', *Methodist Newsletter*, January, 2003.

8. For this reading see Schreiter, *The Ministry of Reconciliation*, pp 70-82.

9. See Shreiter, *Reconciliation*, p 52.

10. See Ed Maloney, *A Secret History of the IRA*, Penguin Books, 2003.

11. Roy Garland, *Gusty Spence*, Blackstaff Press, 2001, pp 170-1.

CHAPTER FIVE

1. Volf in 'A Vision of Embrace', op. cit.

2. *The New Yorker*, Oct 14 & 21, 2002, p 195.

3. Ian Linden, 'The Church and Genocide: Lessons from the Rwandan Tragedy' in Eds Baum and Wells, *The Reconciliation of Peoples*, p 52.

4. Ralph R. Premdas, 'The Church and Reconciliation in Ethnic Conflicts: The Case of Fiji' in Eds Baum and Wells, op. cit., p 93.

5. Duncan Morrow, Derek Birrell, John Greer and Terry O'Keefe, *The Church and Inter-Community Relationships*, Centre for the Study of Conflict, University of Ulster, 1994, p 261.

6. Lewis Mudge, source unknown.

7. The Jewish philosopher Emmanuel Levinas speaks of God in terms of that which is 'different and strange'.

8. From a Cornerstone Community leaflet, 2002.

9. See reference 9, p 222, De Gruchy, *Reconciliation*.

10. Irish Inter-Church Meeting, *Sectarianism: A Discussion Document*, Belfast, 1993, p 100.

11. De Gruchy, *Reconciliation*, p 111.

12. Liechty and Clegg, *Moving Beyond Sectarianism*, p 331.

13. Ibid., p 340.

14. Ibid., p 341.

15. Eds, Baum and Wells, *The Reconciliation of People*, p 191.

16. Keith Clements, *The Churches in Europe as Witnesses to Healing*, WCC Publications, 2003, p 58.

17. Ibid.

18. Ibid.

CHAPTER SIX

1. The painting by the artist Jasper Johns of the US flag, simply entitled *Flag*, suggests the complexity of these symbolic narratives. For Jasper's *Flag* is full of stories. Under its soft, waxy, rough-smooth surface are headlines and stories clipped out of newspapers, barely visible in reproduction. In the gallery, the stories are dimly read through ghostly suspensions of white between red bars. Their spectral presence suggests that under the surface of the flag's straightforward iconic presence are complicated situations, happenings and secrets. The simple banner conceals a complex reality.

2. Quoted in *Remembrance and Forgetting*.

3. Quoted in Ed Vulliamy, *Season in Hell: Understanding Bosnia's War*, St Martin's Press, 1994, p 51.

4. Quoted in *Remembrance and Forgetting*.

5. Ibid.

6. Ignatieff, *The Warrior's Honor*, p 177.

7. Quoted in *Remembrance and Forgetting*.

8. Alan Falconer, 'Remembering' in Eds Falconer and Leichty, *Reconciling Memories*, p 13.

9. 'Reconciling the Histories of Protestants and Catholics in Northern Ireland' in Eds Falconer and Leichty, *Reconciling Memories*.

10. Or the victims may be dead, literally reduced to silence and unable to speak. The German conceptualist artist Jochen Gertz seeks to recall the Jewish dead of Germany in his paradoxical public art: names signed on a column, which sinks slowly into the earth, cobblestones lifted and inscribed with the names of vanished synagogues.

11. Elie Wiesel, *The Fifth Son,* Penguin Books, 1987, p 220.

12. Seamus Deane, *Reading in the Dark,* Jonathan Cape, 1996, p 43.

13. Tom Garvin, Meath Peace Group Talk, October 1997. See www. geocities.com/meathgroup/index.html

14. Terence McCaughey, in Ed Biggar, *Bury the Past,* p 258.

15. Quoted in Priscilla B. Hayner, *Unspeakable Truths,* p 187.

16. See Giles Tremlett, 'Spain's Civil War Comes Back to Life', *The Guardian,* March 8, 2003.

17. Stanley Harakas, 'Forgiveness and Reconciliation: An Orthodox Perspective' in Eds Helmick and Petersen, *Forgiveness and Reconciliation,* p 72.

18. See her essay, 'Northern Ireland: Commemoration, Elegy, Forgetting', in Ed Ian McBride, *History and Memory in Modern Ireland,* Cambridge University Press, 2001.

19. Sir Kenneth Bloomfield, *We Will Remember Them,* Belfast, April 1998, p 11.

20. Jane Leonard, *Memorials to the Casualties of Conflict Northern Ireland,* NI Community Relations Council, Belfast, 1997, p 33.

21. Geiko Mueller-Fahrenholz, 'Deep Remembering – The Art of Forgiveness', unpublished paper, 17th Annual Ministry Conference at Corrymeela, 1997.

22. Ignatieff, *The Warrier's Honor,* p 186.

23. Colm Tóibín, 'The Cause That Called You', *The New York Review of Books,* December 19, 2002.

24. Quoted in *The Church and Nation Report of the Church of Scotland,* Edinburgh, 1998, p 54.

25. Volf, *Exclusion and Embrace,* pp 250-1.

26. Mueller-Fahrenholz, *The Art of Forgiveness,* p 32.

27. John Paul Lederach 'Beyond Violence: Building Sustainable Peace' in Ed Arthur Williamson, *Beyond Violence: The Role of Voluntary and Community Action in Building a Sustainable Peace in Northern Ireland,* NI Community Relations Council and Centre for Voluntary Action Studies, University of Ulster, 1995, p 21.

28. Quoted in *Experience the Power to Change,* Dublin and Belfast, 2001, pp 57-59.

29. Quoted in an article by Kathy Sheridan, *The Irish Times,* January 25, 2002.

30. Brandon Hamber, 'How Should We Remember? Issues to Consider when Establishing Commissions and Structures for Dealing with the Past', unpublished paper presented at the Dealing with the Past: Reconciliation Processes and Peacebuilding Conference, Belfast, 1998.

31. Kenneth Kaunda, *Kaunda on Violence,* London, 1980, p 180.

32. Shriver, *Forgiveness and Politics,* p 54.

33. Shriver, *An Ethic for Enemies,* p 173.

34. Ibid., p 193.

35. Vincent Harding, 'So Much History, So Much Future: Martin Luther

King Jr and the Second Coming of America' in Ed Michael V. Namerato, *Have We Overcome? Race Relations since Brown*, University of Mississippi, 1979, pp 75-76.

36. Jonathan Sachs, *The Dignity of Difference: How to Avoid the Clash of Civilisations*, Continuum, 2002, p 190.

37. Jones, *Embodying Forgiveness*, p 50.

38. See Alastair MacIntyre, *After Virtue*, Duckworth, 1981.

39. Mueller-Fahrenholz, *The Art of Forgiveness*, p 30.

40. See Digeser, *Political Forgiveness*, pp 161-167.

41. Shriver, *An Ethic for Enemies*, p 108.

42. Mueller-Fahrenholz, *The Art of Forgiveness*, pp 74-75.

43. Ed Vulliamy, *The Observer*, December 15, 2002.

44. Schimmel, *Wounds Not Healed by Time*, p 204.

45. Ibid., p 205.

46. Ignatieff, op. cit., pp 186-7.

47. Ed. Biggar, op. cit., p 279.

48. Ibid.

49. Stanley Cohen, *States of Denial: Knowing About Atrocities and Suffering*, Polity Press, 2001, pp 227-8.

50. *Healing Through Remembering: The Report of the Healing Through Remembering Project*, Belfast, 2002.

51. The actions of the British State in Northern Ireland raise the question: How far does State security override legal and moral rules in the interest of defeating deadly enemies such as the Provisional IRA? A state must be held to higher standards than terrorist organisations, otherwise the state becomes, in the words of St Augustine, 'organised brigandage'. The rule of law and moral distinctions between actors collapse. On the other hand, there is a danger of holding the State to an impossible moral perfectionism (which some human rights activists do). The reality is that politicians constantly fail and engage in wrongdoing (if only by omission or because decisions often involve choices between evils) and this is why the issue of forgiveness in politics is important – political life has to keep going and not be paralysed by past wrongdoing. However, the State and its agents have to be held to account. At a minimum if dirty wars are dirty, we are entitled to know how dirty. And the exclusive concern should not be on the misdeeds of the State. We should see wrongdoing in the round. To further complicate the ethical issues involved in the dirty war in Northern Ireland: did out of the stalemate produced by the dirty war emerge the Peace Process?

52. Quotations in this paragraph from Rosie Cowan, *The Guardian*, February 19, 2003.

53. Interview with President Havel, *The Guardian*, March 13, 1999.

54. 'Politics as a Vocation', pp 125-6.

55. Note the words of Garret FitzGerald, former Taoiseach of the Republic of Ireland, about the Northern Ireland Peace Process:
'From the start to finish a striking feature of the whole prolonged Peace

Process has been the prevalence of ambiguity in every aspect of what has been done. Ambiguity about the relationship between the IRA and Sinn Féin, ambiguity about the commitment to decommissioning; ambiguity about the meaning of the ceasefire; ambiguity between successive Irish governments and Sinn Féin.' And then he goes on to argue: 'The last truth is that without all this literally demoralising ambiguity we would not have come to the point where 35 years of continuous violence in the North and 80 years of sporadic violence in our own State that has cost the lives of politicians and many members of the security forces is about to end.' He speaks about the necessity for 'the governments of the two States to pursue what in fact became a very murky path of compromise.' Thus ambiguity, fictions and moral murk have been necessary on the way to peace. Nevertheless we should note Fitzgerald's conclusion: there comes a time 'for the game to end' (*The Irish Times,* April 12, 2003). Constructive ambiguity may make it possible for adversaries to work together and for trust to be built. However, there reaches a stage where ambiguity hinders rather than facilitates trust. Making war and peace involve uneasy ethical choices (see reference 51).
56. Hamber, op. cit.

CHAPTER SEVEN

1. Adam Seligman, *The Problem of Trust,* Princeton University Press, 1997, p 1.
2. Ashutosh Varshney, *Ethnic Conflict and Civil Life: Hindus and Muslims in India,* Yale University Press, 2002.

CONCLUDING REFLECTIONS

1. Philippe Moreau Defarges, *Repentance et Reconciliation,* Presses de Sciences, Po, 1999.
2. Helmick & Petersen, 'A Theology of Forgiveness: Terminology, Rhetoric and the Dialectic of Interfaith Relations', in Eds Helmick and Petersen, p 2.
3. Mueller-Fahrenholz, *The Art of Forgiveness,* p 44.
4. Hannah Arendt, op.cit., pp 238ff.

ANDREW
McNEILE